Africans and African Americans Divided:

The Male-Female African and African American Digital Divide

Ron Farris

Africans and African Americans Divided: The Male-Female African and African American Digital Divide

by Ron Farris

ISBN: 978-1-4357-0272-1

Author Contact Information:

Ron Farris

7635 N La Cholla Blvd., PMB 140

Tucson, Arizona 85741 U.S.A.

Telephone: (520) 907-8250

E-mail: ronaldfarris@netzero.net

SYNOPSIS

This book is about the "Digital Divide". Africans including Africans and African Americans living in the United States have no access to technology. Information technology has been growing at such a fast pace that the world has become divided into information haves and have-nots. White people of middle and upper income are the information haves and African and African American males are primarily the have-nots. Digital Divide, in simple terms refers to the difference in the amount of information and communication technology people of various origins and incomes have between each other and is a predatory discriminative animal which needs to be put to death. There are hundreds of millions of African and African American males throughout the world without access to technology basics. Almost everyone else has access to technology with ease and simplicity. Arguments regarding basic necessities before technology are absurd. There are abundant supplies and resources throughout the world to provide everyone with enough to eat as well as provide them with sophisticated technology so that these people can strive to resolve their issues through the use of computer systems and information and communication technology and the sharing of ideas and information and through opportunities that are provided with the ability to obtain and use good technology. News of life threatening phenomena such as disease and disaster fly through the airwaves and telephone lines at the speed of light and are directed to almost every white person in the universe leaving them with valuable time and opportunity to protect and prepare themselves from such disasters. There is only sparse technology access throughout Africa and in the homes of African and African Americans throughout the United States. This technological sparseness leaves the African and African American people at a distinct and deadly disadvantage and this digital inequity must be considered as an emergency in need of immediate rectification to aid the under-cherished in their fight against the severe issues that they face head on a daily basis.

Much of the information collected for this book is from a compilation of papers I wrote for research study as a graduate student at Columbia University, New York, NY while working in an intensive masters degree program in Computers and Technology in Education. In my research there regarding the Digital Divide the African and African American male was continuously at the bottom of the list when it came to access to technology. I found this quite revolting. What is worse is my discovery that the African and African American male's statistics are no longer improving. The African and African American females gap in the Digital Divide has been steadily closing over the years, yet the African and African American male has stopped improving albeit heading for reversal. I have found research that points to the African and African American females' abilities to take on more difficult coursework throughout their primary and secondary education as a direct relationship to more of the females going on to college over the male and this may very well be a consequence of the African and African American male-female digital divide.

Research studies also indicate that the African and African American males' abilities in taking on more difficult course work can be significantly improved by the availability of technology and their ability and willingness to take advantage of it. Thereby the Digital Divide issue needs to be openly addressed by both public and private resources to impact the African and African American males' access and success with technology. Bridging the Digital Divide as a moral issue is a chance for us to have a tremendous impact on guiding the world to becoming technically noble in that it is committed to fairness, equality, and respectfulness to all regardless of heterogeneity or sameness.

INTRODUCTION

Africans and African Americans have been victims of diversity throughout history. Countless instances of inequality are well documented throughout both world and American history, yet the research of this book has determined that the African and African American, in particular the African and African American male, is the victim of another inequality, the Digital Divide, and since they are victim of such diversity, why cannot this problem be addressed and corrected. The intent of this book is to inform and empower the world. Let us follow proven methodologies to take action to help the African and African American male reach an equal if not superior technological status within our population. African

and African American females are already making powerful
and compelling improvements in decreasing the Digital
Divide that exists within their race and gender and
therefore I assert that we citizens of the world must work
together to help the African and African American male as
well regarding the Digital Divide problem.

CONTENTS

Evidence of African and African American Inequality-
Chapter 3 provides evidence as to why the African
and African American people are being discriminated
against through lack of technology access.

Fear of Technology-Chapter 4 describes problems
related to and why people are afraid of technology.

Anonymity With Digital Technology-Chapter 5
describes new research going on regarding prejudice
and ethnicity and how it relates to the Digital Divide
issue.

Why African and African American Males-Chapter 6
explains how the African and African American male
is at the very bottom of the list when it comes to
access to technology and it explains why this is
happening.

African and African American Technology Achievers-
Chapter 10 gives biographical information regarding
famous African American male technology inventors
and achievers.

World Wide Access Issues-Chapter 11 covers issues
regarding areas of the world that are in need of
technology and why the plans that are in place now
need to be improved upon and accelerated to help
those in need of the technology now.

New Technology-This chapter tells us about the latest
technology available and how and when it will be
used to help with the Digital Divide issue.

Conclusion-Chapter 13 is a summary of the issues
and tells us what needs to be done to help with the
Digital Divide issue.

Chapter 1

Negative Effects of Life Without Technology

Plagued are those that live life without technology. Life without access to technology is all but non-existent amongst white Americans throughout the world and they are continually reaping the benefits of it. White computer users are offered the certain luxury of easy and reliable access to the Internet and it's many benefits and have already restructured the world to rely on this technology to a tremendous degree at much to their advantage. Actually, the Internet technology available to the average household helps that household reap tremendous benefits, including reduced pricing for goods and services as well as the availability of a wider variety of goods and services that are not available to those households or groups without the technology available to them. The purpose of the technology is to use it to benefit those with the technology available. To have the technology not available to people of diverse or economic disadvantage is possibly the worst form of discrimination that the technology creates and this issue needs to be addressed at the highest levels of government to help the African and African American male get what he needs to be a competent and loyal citizen of the world.

A poll by National Public Radio, the Kaiser Family Foundation, and Harvard's Kennedy School of Government has found that the majority of Americans feel that computers and the Internet have made Americans' lives better. This study relates to many citations on how White Americans in the upper income ranges have overwhelmingly rich access to the Internet and computer technology and the racial differences regarding who gets access to technology is disgraceful. Digital discrimination in homes is rampant. Internet access is hugely divided by race in the homes of America. The resources of African and African American males are lacking in many areas of American society primarily due to their not having the same opportunities as other Americans. No access to the Internet or computer technology puts them at a distinct disadvantage. In order to better themselves people need to be competitive with technology. At first glance, not having a PC in ones home seems trivial and non-consequential, however the financial rewards of technology are many. The ability to perform computer aided functions such as writing a neat resume with a PC software program, doing a simple search for employment over the Internet, the ability to pursue academic goals through online coursework, access to financial information and e-mail and fax capabilities shows that the African and African American male is at a distinct disadvantage as compared to those who have access. There is a gap of 11 percentage points between

African and African Americans and White Americans using computers at work, but there is even a larger gap, 22 percentage points, between African and African Americans (52%) and White Americans (73%) who have a computer at home and a similar gap is prevalent in terms of Internet access as well, while African and African American kids (44%) are considerably less likely to use a computer at home than White American kids (76%).

Percentage of computer useage.

Percent of Difference	21%
White Americans w' Computer at Home	73%
African Americans w' Computer at Home	52%
Percent of Difference	32%
White American Kids w' Computer at Home	76%
African American Kids w' Computer at Home	44%

Computers have provided their predominantly white households with the ability to effectively achieve a better lifestyle by keeping track of their families finances and generating extra income by creating new jobs from their homes, as well as improving their ability to retrieve and store important information, and an unlimited list of other advantageous experiences that the African and African American male does not have access to.

Workers with computer skills are able to command significantly higher wages than those without. According to the Economic Research & Data Publications Economic Letter published by the Bank of San Francisco called "The Computer Evolution" estimated that in the year 2001 computer users made 19.2% more in wages than non-skilled computer users in their occupations leaving Africans and African Americans with a lower income on the average. The world is full of new ideas and unlimited diversity and access to the Internet allows for the white households to have access to this. Information on government elections, new laws and also the ability to use the technology to make their feelings, wants, and desires on these issues known to government leaders leaves the African and African American male at a huge disadvantage politically and also without a voice within their own government. Technology is used in white households to maintain an understanding of the world that they live in and to understand the lifestyles, customs and values of other people from around the world to maintain what is known as a mainstream attitude where it is possible for them to adjust and maintain alignment with people everywhere. The African and African American male is left alone to look at the world from what he sees around him and does not understand the significant differences in culture because he does not have the technology that white people have.

Non-exposure to computer technology within the household or at school or work has left the African and African American male in fear and alienation of the technology. This fear is very close to the same fear and alienation some people have of snakes and other scary creatures. If the African and African American male fear the technology then he will not have the ability to take advantage of it.

The African and African American male who doesn't have access to computer technology in his home is a victim of proprietorship. He is victimized by his lack of resources and denied the self-esteem provided to the white families with access to this valuable resource. This self-esteem is valuable when seeking employment, where the white person can put his or her name along with an e-mail address on their job application, while the African and African American male must admit that he does not have an e-mail address and thusly appears as a less likely candidate for the position he is applying for. There is also the issue of him having to ask for 3rd party assistance to have a resume done or to write a nicely typed letter to send to an employer.

Negative forces related to minorital ownership of technology are making it difficult for the African and African American male to prioritize technology as something that is an absolute necessity to succeed in the computerized world we live in. If the majority of African and African American males do not have the technology available to them, it is difficult for them to find the value in the ownership of the technology.

The African and African American male child does not have the same ability as white children have to do his school homework on a home based computer with access to the Internet. His ability to research his homework assignments is negatively hindered and therefore he might receive lower grades on his homework assignments and does not have available to him a magnificent learning resource that white children have long been afforded and find to be intellectually stimulating and easy to access with information available to them with a click of a button.

Therefore his abilities are muted and he is left searching his world around him for answers to questions that just are not available without the technological resources available to white children. College is much the same for the African and African American male. He has little or no access to technology anywhere except what is available to the general student population that is provided by the college, which he is attending. Usually these resources are continually full and have limited hours of use which again leaves the African and African American male without the same opportunities as white and other students who have the technology available to them in their home or dormitory room thusly leaving him stranded and without hope while the other students are moving swiftly with technology when completing their assignments. Finding information about colleges the African and African American male may wish to attend requires a great deal of time and effort and using technology requires less time and effort then accessing the information without the technology. Access to scholarship information and grants and loans is readily available on the Internet and without the technology to access this information it is very difficulty to find this information and once the information is found, even more difficult and time consuming to apply for it.

There is also research available on a subject that points to various prejudicial effects felt by African and African American male students that white students and others are not subject to due to the white student readily having access to technology and that subject is anonymity. Aside from the issues regarding marketing and technology that can get an Internet users personal information by spying on your home computer while you are on the Internet, the amount one reveals about his or herself is controlled by the user of the technology leaving that person basically anonymous. This anonymity is valuable in ways that are not that obvious. For instance, studies have shown that students of other then white ethnic origin often perform better while taking distance learning program classes and that the more anonymous students of other then white ethnic origin are, the better they perform on their coursework. African and African Americans perform better through technology over being in a traditional classroom where their physical presence is required. It is thought that because their teachers and fellow students have no way of knowing what they look like, if they are African and African American or Chinese American and many times even if they are male or female. A recent study published in the online edition of "Nature Neuroscience" determined through the use of brain imaging (fMRI), which measures brain activity, that when people of white ethnicity are in the presence of African and African American people that problem solving skills diminish within the white individual. The reason for the diminished mental resources was determined to be due to the white individuals suppression of racial bias. The suppression of racial bias apparently exhausts mental resources. There research found that brain activity changed when responding to the faces of and African American individuals. A synopsis of the Dartmouth study is available at:http://www.dartmouth.edu/~news/releases/2003/11/1 7.html in the Dartmouth News.

It is has not yet been assessed whether the same diminishment of mental capacity occurs when African and

African Americans are exposed to white Americans and there are many other interesting artifacts to collect from this type of study including as to whether distance learning over the Internet would produce the same results in a controlled laboratory experiment rather then surveyed from their homes and offices. There being no face to face interaction in most distance learning courses, these types of studies point to conclusions that African and African American males improve there learning experiences with distance learning technology and if this is the case then here is another reason why the African and African American male is a victim of digital diversity that can be improved by providing him with adequate resources.

As a whole and in conclusion to this chapter, African and African American males are victimized without mercy by their lack of access to technology, which can improve their lives substantially. There are other issues at play here that leave the African and African American male as an ongoing victim of the Digital Divide and who is making no headway against this violent storm of extreme prejudice that leaves

them jobless, homeless, or living a life of crime to survive

and leaving them with no desire to improve themselves in

any way.   In the next chapter we will discuss some of the

positive aspects of technology access.

Chapter 2

Positive Effects of Life With Technology

Positive effects of technology to the African and African American male are multiple and permanent. The African and African American male with computer skills and access to the Internet would have access to an infinite amount of information already available to white people everywhere. With computer skills they could write resumes and with e-mail make contact with companies in foreign lands, they would have access to translation programs that would allow them to read news and to translate information into whatever language which they want to communicate in and could also teach their

selves how to speak foreign languages and make friends
with others from technologically sophisticated societies that
would assist the African and African American male in
getting assistance in providing a support system for
themselves. Once everyone everywhere has the technology
available and is knowledgeable in it's use, then many more
issues could be resolved. Some of the advantages that a
technologically sophisticated society could implement are
entities such as a world voting system where issues that
demand world cooperation and resources are easily
identified and real problems that are effecting certain areas
can be served by the appropriate society with the help of
world-wide attention to the issue. In areas where telephone
access is not available there are innumerable police and
medical emergencies that are not responded to promptly or
not at all undoubtedly due to the lack of technology that is
available everywhere else. Improvements in productivity of
businesses and industry are often associated with
increases in technology. Offering up-to-date technology to a

technologically impoverished nation could create a competitive advantage that makes it a desirable place for companies to do business which in business terms means jobs and improvement of the countries' economy. Access to the Internet in rural areas also increases the chances that a business will go there and offers the African and African American male more chances to have a career and the more businesses that are in an area provides more opportunities for community and technological growth. Schools have online programs available where little or no time is spent on campus and the entire learning takes place through a personal computer with an Internet connection with professors that hold classes on the Internet. Teachers can also implant technology into their curriculum providing a better educational environment with access to the world rather than only the world around them. There are many projects that allow teachers to build web pages at no cost and implement and publish their teaching ideas to be shared with other teachers and students around the world.

The Department of Economic and Social Affairs are currently working on initiatives to develop Internet connectivity into disparaged areas around the world, the United Nations Information and Communication Technologies (ICT) Task Force and the Wireless Internet Institute are instituting policies to devise state of the art wireless technology systems to provide worldwide universal Internet connectivity.

In 2002, the Secretary-General of the United Nations said that we need to think of ways to bring wireless-fidelity applications to the developing world so as to make use of unlicensed radio spectrum to deliver cheap and fast Internet access. Private sector funding, expertise, and technological development from companies such as IBM and Intel is to be united with public government resources to accelerate the implementation of broadband wireless Internet in under served areas of the world. As an expert in the field of broadband communication and networking I am afraid that the United Nations is mistaken in their wireless approach in providing worldwide universal Internet connectivity due to the undeniable fact that fiber optic cable technology can be installed at a fraction of the cost of Satellite wireless technology and it can be implemented at a much faster rate and has much higher performance standards then satellite. The new technology of accessing the Internet through regular power lines is now becoming available which could work as an add-too option to the electrical infrastructure that may be already present in many countries who do not have a satisfactory telephone communication infrastructure to implement affordable Internet access in it yet may have electrical power lines and households have access to electricity therefore being capable of using their electrical outlets for Internet access. If you are interested in Satellite vs. Fibreoptic/electrical lines subject you may want to pick up my new book "Undivided, Lessons Regarding World-Wide Access to Digital Technology" which will provide you with much more information on this subject.

To continue on, four series of issues have been outlined to complete the agenda of the initiative in time for the second phase of the World Summit on the Information Society (WSIS). They include: -- National Regulator Capacity-Building – Global Wireless Internet and Local Authorities – Wireless Internet and the Arab World – Wireless Internet and African Continent.

Overseen by a multinational, multidisciplinary advisory board, the four series will research the needs and many technical and financial aspects of providing this wireless Internet technology to all.   This unique program comes after one year of successful collaboration between W2i and UN ICT Task Force. The two bodies co-hosted a conference in June, 2003 at the United Nations Headquarters called "The Wireless Internet Opportunity for Developing Countries", featuring panelists and brainstorm sessions with wireless Internet and ICT-for-development stakeholders from around the world.

The UN ICT Task Force, W2i, and a program implemented by the World Bank released a book at the World Summit on Information Society in Geneva, in which the Secretary General of the United Nations wrote it is precisely in places where no infrastructure exists that Wi-Fi can be particularly effective, helping countries to leapfrog generations of telecommunications technology and infrastructure to empower their people. Bringing together international organizations such as the European Commission, the United Nations Development Programme (UNDP), the United Nations Institute for Training and Research (UNITAR), the World Bank, the Inter-American Development Bank, and regional and local professional organizations such as the Wi-Fi Alliance and the WiMax Forum UN ICT Task Force and W2i have pulled together a broad base to support the initiative. A global atmosphere is established by the UN ICT Task Force in it's bringing together of resources to span the globe with Internet access and ending the digital divide, creating digital good fortune and thusly firmly put ICT at the service of development for all. The Task Force has forged a strategic partnership between the United Nations system, private industry, financing trusts and foundations, donors, program countries and other relevant players.

The Wireless Internet Institute is an international, independent think tank started in the year 2001 fostering, international, independent think tank in pursuit of bringing wireless Internet providing wireless Internet Launched in 2001, the Wireless Internet Institute is an international, independent think tank bringing wireless Internet players together to accelerate the adoption of wireless Internet working toward universal connectivity to improve social, economic and educational development around the world. For more information visit www.unicttaskforce.org or www.w2i.org the Internet.

Institutes and initiatives such as the ones described are helpful yet still not enough to improve the emergency situation currently being suffered by the African and

African American male caused by centuries of unequal and unjust treatment. The African and African American male should be prioritized as in greater need then those who are already making substantial gains with the present social assets available to them and provided everything needed to bring them to justice and equality. Technological freedom requires means and access and the skills necessary to make the technology advantageous to its user. The world is not aware of the potential of technology. School research has determined that African and African American boys without access to technology in their homes perform worse academically than the majority of their peers who have technology in their homes. The African and African American male needs to be given the skills and the means to take advantage of the power associated with technology.

African and African American male teachers need to be trained as role models to emulate the positive results that technological freedom provides. Priorities must be put in place to keep the African and African American male student in a technologically free environment where he has access to state of the art computers and communication technology and he is provided with the ability and knowledge to use them to his best advantage. Teachers and role models of all persuasions need access to counseling to help the African and African American male gain a positive technological self-image.

The resulting effects of eliminating the Digital Divide in regards to the African and African American male will improve societies ability to imagine and create new opportunities for everyone. Eliminating the Digital Divide for these people will give the African and African American male a chance to resolve issues rather then being part of the issue that needs resolved. Skills and access to technology will free society of the burdens that have been placed upon the African and African American male in such a way that all of the burdens that have been placed upon him after being a societal scapegoat for so long will be lifted and a new technologically sophisticated society will appear.

Exploration and investigation of discriminatory issues are often washed over and remain hidden because the discriminating society is also the controlling society and it does not want to lose it's advantage that it enjoys over the entity that is being discriminated against.   In our next chapter we will provide evidence of how the controlling white society is technologically discriminating against the African and African American male.

Chapter 3

Evidence of African and African American Inequality

The previous chapter included a brief summary of what is being done at this time to bring Internet access to underdeveloped places in the world as well as information and guidance on what needs to be done to help end the African and African American Digital Divide. This chapter will provide proof that the terrible issue regarding the African and African American Digital Divide is real. Evidence that documents the prejudicial treatment of the African and African American male as unequal and impeded due to his inability to access and use the technology readily available to people of other persuasions and gender is the primary topic of this chapter. The preponderance of evidence pointing to racial and gender prejudice related to the African and African American male and the Digital Divide proves without a shadow of a doubt that the African and African American male has worthy cause for and needs to be given priorital status and assistance within our justice system and world assistance is necessary to address this issue. The following statistics contain certain information that the African and African American is not even close to being an equal in terms of technology.

A study on racial differences done by Hoffman and Novak (1998) found that Whites were significantly more likely to have a computer in their home as well as at work. In addition, the research concluded that Whites were less likely to have ever used the Web at home, whereas African and African Americans were slightly more likely to have ever used the Web at school. It was also determined in this study that whites were still more likely to own a home computer than were African and African Americans and to have used the Web recently, despite differences in education. The study also concluded that the Digital Divide for Web usage was equal when a computer was present in both the African and African Americans and the white households. However, it was determined that white Americans have more resources available to them to gain access to the Web then do African and African Americans and therefore the whites were more likely to have accessed the Web then the African and African Americans. Another research study done by the United States Commerce Department's National Telecommunications and Information Administration (McConnaughey & Lader, 1998) analyzed data on computer penetration rates from the October 1997 Census Current Population Survey as part of an ongoing examination of the Digital Divide. The study came to the conclusion that between the November 1994 CPS and the one in 1998, the gap between African and

African Americans and whites was actually greater when considering home computer ownership and Internet access. This analysis represented an update from their 1995 study of similar data from the November 1994 Census Current Population Survey and they concluded that between 1994 and 1997 African American households rose from 11.2% to 23.5% since December 1998 in a CPS study. This compares to an overall rise in Internet access by U.S. Households over the same period from 26.2% to 41.5% (or 43.6 million households).

In a graduate report at a Vanderbilt University Study called "The Evolution of the Digital Divide-How Gaps in Internet Access May Impact Electronic Commerce" by Donna L. Hoffman, Thomas P. Novak, and Ann E. Schlosser, it was surveyed here that the relationship between gender and Web access and use for whites and African and African Americans that Web access and use are lower for women than men and that among recent Web users, men are more likely to have been using the Web longer and to have used the Web more recently and that women are more likely to be newer users. The interesting data collected in this study is that while white men are more frequent Web users than white women, African and African American men are not more frequent Web users than African American women. What follows is an analysis of differences by race for each gender. The study shows that in the Men category, white men consistently are more likely to have access to the Web as well as to have ever used the Web and to have owned a PC at home more than African American men and that these differences have continued over time. White men owning a PC at home has grown for white men, yet not for the African American male. White men are slightly more likely to have PC access at work. Among recent Web users, African American men are much more likely than white men to be newer Web users and this finding persists over time. White men were more than three times as likely as African American men to have been online for two years or more (20.31 percent versus

6.20 percent), where fifty percent of white and African American men had been online that long.

Percentage of New Web Using: White Males vs. New African and African American Males

White Males	African and African American Male
6.20 Percent	20.31 Percent

According to the report White Males were more likely to be the most recent Web users than African and African American men at a percentage rate of 65.46 percent for White Males as compared to 37.04 percent for the African and African American Male.

Percentage of More Recent Web Usage: White Males vs. African and African American Males

White Males	African and African American Male
65.46 Percent	37.04 Percent

White men were also more frequent Web users than African American men at a rate of 55.94 percent versus 38.9 percent even though later studies have shown an increase by both White Males and African and African American males.

Percentage of More Frequent Web Usage: White Males vs. New   African and African American males

White Males	African and African American Male
55.94 Percent	38.9 Percent

The study asserts that over time, the percentage of African and African American men ever using the Web at home, work, school or other locations has increased considerably and that the percentage of White Males who ever used the Web at school is flat, has grown only in small amounts for home and work, and has fallen for ever used at other locations. African and African American men were more likely to have ever used the Web at school or at other locations, compared to White men.

Africans and African Americans Ever Using the Web at Home, School, or Other Locations Increased
The Percentage of White Males Who Ever Used the Web at School is Flat

Increase and decrease of Web useage.

Also this same study concluded that White women are more likely than African American women to have access to the Web as well as to have ever used the Web, to own a PC and to have PC access at work and these differences have persisted over time. As for men, the percentage of women owning PCs at home has increased over time for white women, but not African American women however not to as great an extent as the difference between White Males and African and African American males and also African and African American women were much more likely than White women to be new users, but over time this difference has disappeared showing that the African and African American woman has become equal with White women and the Digital Divide no longer exists amongst them in this particular area.

Chapter 4

Fear of Technology

Technology can be a perplexing and fearful thing, especially for the African and African American male. Lack of training and African and African American technological role models, as well as lack of access to technology creates a psychological obstacle for the African and African American male to overcome. Gentle preparation tactics for the African and African American male must be implemented by teachers and instructors who have been educated and specially trained as to the special needs of the African and African American male. Identity and self-esteem issues specific to the African and African American male must be addressed so that the

African and African American male has a positive focus while he is in training and that he will continue on his high-tech journey with positive associations with technology when he leaves the training environment and therefore will continue using the technological skills he was trained in throughout his lifetime to help overcome obstacles and issues that befall him.

African and African American males are not the only people capable of having a fear of technology. I recall my early college days when taking my first computer programming class. Initially I was excited and filled with pride upon the thought of being a skilled computer programmer. It was my first times to ever be near a computer and I was working with one of the most advanced state of the art mainframe computers of its time. I thought programming would be fun, however I soon found out how difficult it was. It wasn't just typing in information into the computer to be processed, as I had previously believed and the complexity of using the mainframe and computer programming left me dumbfounded. I had to learn an entire computer language (BASIC), which now is simple to me yet when I first began to program was the most difficult and perplexing task that had ever been placed before me. Just starting up the application I needed to enter a program into the mainframe was difficult and using the various computer software tools associated with a mainframe computer share was far beyond what my previous idea of programming was like. I had to become immediately proficient at things I had never even heard of before. I was totally overwhelmed and I must say frustrated and frightened and my teacher was not aware of the terror I was experiencing. I was afraid and highly capable of making a mistake with the computer. I dropped this class. However, I later continued on with my computer studies and eventually earned a degree in information systems. With every computer class I took though, I still experienced the same fear of technology and the only way I could reach the next level of computer programming was to become an expert at the previous computer skills that I learned and build upon my previous experiences with new technical experiences. Learning by building upon past experience is referred to as the constructive learning theory and is now the most favored method of teaching in schools around the world.

Constructive learning experiences allowed me to change my fear into excitement when facing new challenges related to technology rather than allowing fear to shut me down not allowing me to proceed in this strange new technologically advanced world. Constructive learning should be emphasized in all instruction made available to fight the African and African American male Digital Divide. Technology can remove barriers related to the African and African American male Digital Divide that are of an internal nature to the human design and technology also aids in areas that are uncontrollable by the individual without the interdiction and use of technology. The next chapter reveals some of the new and exciting research related to ethnicity and prejudice that is being done at one of our higher institutions of learning that is related to the African and African American male Digital Divide.

Chapter 5

Anonymity With Digital Technology

Advanced technology allows users to be heard and seen at times and places that they wish to be seen at rather then be seen as how and where they really are. The anonymity of online classrooms allow students and teachers to control how much they reveal about themselves as compared to traditional classrooms. They need not reveal the color of their skin, their age or whether they are handicapped or not.

There is laboratory research being done now that points to various prejudicial effects felt by African and African American male students that White students and teachers taking part in traditional classes are not subject to. In the case of the White students and teachers, this is due to their majorital and predominant status in the classrooms. Anonymity is available in online classrooms that is not available in the traditional classroom environment. Aside from the issues regarding marketing and technology that can reveal an Internet users personal information by spying on your home computer while you are on the Internet, the amount one reveals about his or herself is controlled by the user of the technology leaving that person basically anonymous. This anonymity is valuable in ways that are not yet apparent. A recent study at Dartmouth University determined through the use of brain imaging (fMRI) equipment which measures brain activity, that when people of White ethnicity are in the presence of African and African American male people that problem solving skills diminish within the White individuals. Also, studies have shown that students of other then White ethnic origin often perform better while taking distance learning program classes and that the more anonymous students of other then White ethnic origin are, the better they perform on their coursework. African and African Americans perform better through technology then they perform in a traditional classroom where their physical presence is required. In my opinion it is because there teachers and fellow students have no way of knowing what they look like, if they are African and African American or Chinese American and many times even if they are male or female. A recent study published in the online edition of "Nature Neuroscience" determined through the use of brain imaging (fMRI), which measures brain activity, that when people of White ethnicity are in the presence of African and African-American people that problem solving skills diminish within the White individual. The reason for the diminished mental resources was determined to be due to the White individuals suppression of racial bias. The suppression of racial bias apparently exhausts mental resources.

What follows is a synopsis of the study from the *Dartmouth News:* New study: Interracial interactions are cognitively demanding Dartmouth College Office of Public Affairs • Press Release Posted 11/17/03

A new Dartmouth study reveals that interracial contact has a profound impact on a person's attention and performance. The researchers found new evidence using brain imaging that White individuals attempt to control racial bias when exposed to African individuals, and that this act of suppressing bias exhausts mental resources. Published in the online edition of "Nature Neuroscience" on Nov. 16, the study combines the use of functional magnetic resonance imaging (fMRI), which measures brain activity, with other behavioral tests common to research in social and cognitive psychology to determine how White individuals respond to African individuals.

Their findings suggest that harboring racial bias, however unintentional, makes negotiating interracial interactions more cognitively demanding. Similar to the depletion of a muscle after intensive exercise, the data suggest that the demands of the interracial interaction result in reduced capacity to engage in subsequent cognitive tasks, say the researchers.

For the study, thirty White individuals were measured for racial bias, which involved a computer test to record the ease with which individuals associate White American and African American racial groups with positive and negative concepts. Racial bias is measured by a pattern in which individuals take longer to associate the White Americans with negative concepts and African Americans with positive concepts. The study participants then interacted with either an African or a White individual, and afterward they were asked to complete an unrelated cognitive task in which they had to inhibit instinctual responses. In a separate fMRI session, these individuals were presented with photographs of unfamiliar African male and White male faces, and the activity of brain regions thought to be critical to cognitive control was assessed.

According to Richeson, most people find it unacceptable to behave in prejudiced ways during interracial interactions and make an effort to avoid doing so, regardless of their level of racial bias. A different research project by Richeson and her colleagues suggested that these efforts could leave individuals temporarily depleted of the resources needed to perform optimally on certain cognitive tasks. This new study by Richeson provides striking evidence that supports the idea that interracial contact temporarily impairs cognitive task performance. These results suggest, according to the researchers, that harboring racial bias in an increasingly diverse society may be bad for one's cognitive performance.

Other authors on the paper include Abigail A. Baird, Assistant Professor of Psychological and Brain Sciences; Heather Gordon, Ph.D. Student in Psychological and Brain Sciences; Todd F. Heatherton, the Champion International Professor of Psychological and Brain Sciences and Director of the Center for Social Brain Sciences at Dartmouth;

Carrie Wyland, Ph.D. Student in Psychological and Brain Sciences; Sophie Trawalter, Ph.D. Student in Psychological and Brain Sciences; and J. Nicole Shelton, Assistant Professor of Psychology at Princeton University.

The National Science Foundation and the Rockefeller Center at Dartmouth College supported this research.

Equality through digital anonymity alone is reason enough to take this African and African American issue off of the back burner of the stove and provide the necessary training and technology to allow the African and African American male the same equality that the predominant White teachers and students enjoy with each other.

African and African American males' have many other issues that keep them Digitally Divided from the rest of the world and in the next chapter we shall discuss factors that are causing the African and American male to remain technologically impeded while the White and other ethnic majorities have succeeded.

Chapter 6

Why Not African and African American Males?

Male Africans and African Americans are discriminated against frequently including in the area referred to as the Digital Divide. The results are in and they show that Africans and African Americans ever using the Web at home, school, or other places have increased and the percentage of White males who ever used the Web is flat. All White males surveyed have used the Web and all African and African Americans ever to use the web has increased, so therefore the gap in

the Digital Divide is widening between the African and
African American male and white men.

Internet at home and school or other.

African and African Americans Ever Using the Web at Home, School, or Other Locations Increased
The Percentage of White Males Who Ever Used the Web at School is Flat

Also this same study concluded that White women are
more likely than African American women to have access to
the Web as well as to have ever used the Web, to own a PC
and to have PC access at work and these differences have
persisted over time. As for men, the percentage of women
owning PCs at home has increased over time for White
women, but not African American women however not to as
great an extent as the difference between White Males and
African American males and also African American women
were much more likely than White women to be new users,
but over time this difference has disappeared showing that
the African American woman has become equal with White
women and the Digital Divide no longer exists amongst

them in this particular area. Gaps in digital inequality can be caused by lack of opportunity, lack of training or education, lack of interest or understanding of the benefits of technology or perhaps because white people do not want African and African American males to have this competitive and technically superior edge that is so overwhelmingly enjoyed by White people in society. Outreach to the African and African American male must occur now. Technological freedom and access both in home and public needs to be made available for everyone. African and African American role models from the sports and entertainment fields are beginning to recognize the plight of the digitally diverse African and African American male and are trying to do something about it. There are a large number of philanthropic societies sponsored by the famous and wealthy African and African American celebrities that are raising money in support of the fight against the African and African American male Digital Divide. Celebrities supporting the fight against the African and African American Digital Divide are still not as publicized as other charities, yet we hope that celebrity support continues to increase and the more sports and entertainment personalities seen in ads and promotions using computers and technology, the better it is for the African and African American male who is the most disparaged victim of the Digital Divide.

Here are some of the charities related specifically to ending the Digital Divide:

American Computer Foundation

Bridging the digital divide

PO Box 540589

154 Moody St

Waltham, MA 02454

http://www.crpic.org

Mission and Programs

Mission

The American Computer Foundation (ACF) inherited a legacy of innovation and entrepreneurship from its roots in the Boston Computer Society. Since 1997, innovative thinking and action have driven the ACF's contributions to establish equal access to the social and economic benefits of information technology. The ACF staff and Board nurture the talent of community-based technology center personnel by working alongside constituents, business partners and staff to build sustainable programs, workforce training initiatives and, most importantly, collaborations with industry, academia and the nonprofit community.

Programs

(1)Providing free public access to computers, the Internet and basic computer instruction; (2) Acting as a technology resource center for individuals, small businesses, schools, and community organizations; and (3) Offering free or low-cost advanced computer education and job training classes to empower people to more fully participate in today's information economy.

Program / Activities (NTEE Code)

Education N.E.C.

Results

Accomplishments for Fiscal Year Ending 12/31/2003 Established as one of the first organizations to offer the IC3 (Internet and Core Computing Certification) training program and certification testing in greater Boston, consistently observed a usage rate of 1000-1500 people per month from 21 towns in greater Boston in their public access computer lab program.

As a Verizon ePartner, provided grant-funded computer training for employees of nonprofit organizations nationwide.

Objectives for Fiscal Year Beginning 01/01/2004 Broaden outreach for the computer training scholarship program for employees of nonprofit organizations at the CRPIC through the Verizon e-Partner program. Increase the number and variety of low cost/no cost computer classes available to unemployed adults in the greater Boston area through strategic partnerships with the Dept. of Labor and the One Stop Career Centers. Increase the number of middle school age children served at the CRPIC through new program initiatives in collaboration with the Waltham Partnership for Yosuth, the Waltham Public Schools and area youth organizations.

Self-Assessment

The ACF dba CRPIC tracks its effectiveness in the following ways: 1) growth in the number of people using the public access program and community classes 2) feedback from their patrons though evaluation forms, suggestion box, patron comments and letters and website use 3) growth of the operating endowment, 4) number of new inquiries/requests for all the services provided by the CRPIC, 5) and number/size of grants/donations received by the CRPIC Chief Executive Profile .

ACF, Chairman Arthur H. Nelson has founded 17 diverse companies, a collection of 8 corporations and 9 nonprofits organizations ranging from manufacturing (General Electronics Lab), real estate (first executive office park in America with on site child care and an accredited full day kindergarten), social research (AIRINC), education (TERC), entrepreneurial studies, communications (PINet) and civil service. Since 1952 Arthur Nelson has built is companies around the same foundation, the application of technology and innovation to solve social problems.

Mr. Nelson was named a 1999 Ernst and Young Entrepreneur of the Year.

Additional Comments

The American Computer Foundation merged with the Charles River Public Internet Center in December of 2002. The merger brings together the human and financial resources of both organizations.

Byte Back

Providing computer skills to low-income DC area youth and adults

815 Monroe St NE

Washington, DC 20017

http://www.byteback.org

Mission and Programs

Mission

Byte Back partners with organizations and volunteers to provide affordable computer skills to under-served members of the community.

Byte Back empowers, serves the community, builds confidence, educates, and helps people get better jobs.

Programs

Byte Back has five programs that serve the target populations: Community Tech Program, Youth Tech-Partnering, Intern Technology Academy, Fast Track, and Cisco Academy.

Internship Tech Academy

This program prepares students for the technology career ladder! Students spend approximately 18 months in learning and working environment to develop extensive skills in Computer Networking or Web Development. Interns receive ten hours a week of free training in exchange for ten hours of their work, which includes acting as Byte Back site administrators, receptionists, teachers, network assistants, technical support staff, and program assistants. Training is not only technical; job retention skills (soft skills) are included in work assignments. This program is the heart of Byte Back, as it is the Interns who run Byte Back and support all other programs.

This program serves primarily unemployed and low-income adults. They have graduated 38 who now earn between $35,000-70,000! Eight-five percent of students are African American and 55% are female.

Cisco Academy

Cisco Academy is an international training program, which prepares people for industry recognized certification, such as Cisco Certified Networking Administrators (CCNA). Byte Back offers CCNA training to all students in the Intern Tech Academy, which takes 9-12 months for completion. They have had six graduates of Cisco who passed their exams with 90% and above, two of whom are now CCNA certified and working in the IT industry.

Cisco is the world's largest maker of equipment that directs Internet traffic and has academies that train for networking certification around the world. Byte Back is proud to be one of the few Regional Cisco Academies in the Washington, DC area serving adults.

Community Tech Program

Direct Service: This program involves six weeks of computer class instruction once a week for two hours and is taught by their pool of over 600 volunteers. Courses range from beginner to advanced levels, such as the Microsoft Office Suite, HTML, and Dream Weaver. Byte Back offers 25+ classes per week in six-week sessions to as many as 600 students throughout the year.

Indirect Service: Byte Back also partners with other community-based organizations to provide them with volunteer teachers, computer lab set-up, technical support, hands-on objective based curricula, and consulting services. They currently have three full Byte Back partner sites. They are currently seeking a long-term partner in South East DC.

Fast Track Program

A core curriculum of basic hardware and MS Office classes is offered in eight-week sessions, with 72 hours of instruction and hands-on training. Partner sites offering Fast Track include Simpson Hamlin, School of Tomorrow, and Catholic Charities.

In 2002 this program was only offered 3-4 times/year, however, as of July 2003, they provide 4-6 sessions/month at four sites, totaling 27 sessions per year, serving over 240 students! To meet the growing demand for Fast Track, Byte Back needs to recruit and train more instructors, upgrade classroom and lab software and equipment, upgrade and produce instructional materials.

Youth-Tech Partnering

Indirect service: Byte Back partners with youth-serving organizations to provide computer lab set-up, technical support, hands-on objective based curricula, and consulting services. Their Byte Back youth program is partially funded through a three-year Mead Family Foundation grant ($12,000 per year) to document and share their hands-on curricula and develop a resource center.

Direct service: This past summer they trained middle school aged youth from the World Missions Extension Center at their Headquarters. The 12-week course emphasizes responsibility and reliability, while training in HTML and web design.

Program / Activities (NTEE Code)

Vocational Technical

Adult, Continuing Education

Community, Neighborhood Development, Improvement

Results

Accomplishments for Fiscal Year ending 12/31/2002 offered over 100 classes (1200 hours of training) to as many as 600 community students throughout the year.

Served over 240 students through their Fast Track program, an eight-week program that trains students in Windows, Word, Excel, and PC Basics. This is an intensive, 72-hour course. These students are now qualified for basic office jobs and 1/3 of them apply for their Intern Tech Academy.

With support from Cisco, Inc. they have become a Cisco Academy and offer CCNA network training. They have had six graduates of Cisco who passed their exams with 90% and above, two of whom are now CCNA certified and working in the IT industry.

Objectives for Fiscal Year Beginning 01/01/2003 Expand Capacity: To serve more students and organizations by building lasting partnerships.

Pilot-to-Model: To transfer competence to other organizations by continuing to develop, define, and document their policies, procedures, curriculum, and data management systems.

Facility Improvement: To make efficient use of computer labs and workspace in order to provide a professional working environment by creating and implementing a master plan for building maintenance and improvements.

Self-Assessment

Their evaluation system involves collecting both qualitative and quantitative data from questionnaires, surveys, and focus groups. They involve all staff members, volunteers, students, as well as employers, businesses and other stakeholders.

In July 2003 they began an Intern Taskforce, made up of board members who are assessing the state of the Intern Tech Academy. They are conducting interviews with interns, holding focus groups, and gathering input from volunteers and staff members. They will use this information to make improvements to the program.

Chief Executive Profile

A Washington, DC native from a family that has been in the District for generations, Paul understands the community. His professional experience includes thirteen years managing operations for The Hannaford Company (a communications firm). His work in public affairs and community projects is extensive, including everything from organizing neighborhood anti-drug efforts, to staffing a subcommittee for the Congressional Committee on Education and the Workforce.

Additional Comments

Byte Back seeks volunteers who are interested in teaching one 90-minute class a week for a total of 6 weeks. Volunteers are also needed to assist in curriculum development, web development, application development, trouble-shooting, placement assistance, and fund raising.

Persons interested in participating, or for more information, contact Debony Heart at heart@byteback.org.

Computers 4 Kids

Equitable access to technology resources

COMPUTERS 4 KIDS INC

150 E AURORA ST

WATERBURY, CT 06708

Mission and Programs

Mission

SUPPLY COMPUTERS TO NONPROFIT ORGANIZATIONS.

Programs

EXPENSES TO DISTRIBUTE DONATIONS-THE ORGANIZATION DISTRIBUTES COMPUTERS AND COMPUTER ACCESSORIES TO VARIOUS NOT FOR PROFIT EDUCATIONAL INSTITUTIONS TO HELP STUDENTS AND TEACHERS AS A SUPPORT TOOL AS WELL AS FOR ADMINISTRATIVE SUPPORT.

Program / Activities (NTEE Code)

Fund Raising and/or Fund Distribution

Computers for All

Computers for everyone -- no matter their income level

Computers-For-All

5385 Auburn Ln

Portage, MI 49002

http://www.computers-for-all.org

Mission and Programs

Mission

They try to make sure all children and elderly and disadvantaged in their area have the use of their own computer. In this world of technology everyone should have a computer no matter whether they can afford it or not. They offer free upgrades for the life of the computer also.

Programs

Restoring and rebuilding used computers making sure each one is personalized for the person that will be receiving that computer with all licensed software on each computer from educational software to games for the children.

Program / Activities (NTEE Code)

Single Organization Support

Fund Raising and/or Fund Distribution

Results

Accomplishments for Fiscal Year ending 12/31/2002. They donate computers to children so they can do their homework on them.

They donate to the elderly and they get such pleasure out of having their own computer some of them even decide to write down their life histories. They make use of used computers that are still good and otherwise would be thrown away and wasted.

Objectives for Fiscal Year Beginning 01/01/2003. Provide computers for elderly persons.

Provide computers for children so they can expand their education and help to improve their homework skills. Provide a computer to a disadvantaged person needing one for job training or a disabled person needing one for their job placement. Chief Executive Profile

Angela Castellani, President, is currently disabled herself with major back and seizure disorders having had many back surgeries she understands the importance of a helping hand in a time of need. She believes all children and the disadvantaged should have access to their wonderful technologies this world has to offer. She has done a lot of volunteer work through the years. She studied with business as her major at Western Michigan University and has some nursing training from Lake Michigan College. She helped to found the local Animal Meals on Wheels organization, which helps to feed the animals of the elderly and disabled persons pets in their area.

Additional Comments

They are a new organization and are in need of a lot of used computers. They have received recognition from their State Representative Fred Upton as he stated what they are doing is giving low income families an opportunity to improve their lives and to expose low income families to what a computer has to offer them that they otherwise may never have had the opportunity to experience.

Computers for Children

Increasing children's access to computers

COMPUTERS FOR CHILDREN INC

237 MAIN ST STE 400

BUFFALO, NY 14203

Mission and Programs

Mission

To enhance the learning opportunities for children by increasing their access to computers.

Programs Evaluate and assess computer technology needs, provide website development and hosting, as well as provide technical services, troubleshooting and support for schools, educational institutions and other charitable 501(c)(3) institutions dedicated to enhancing the learning opportunities of youth through grants in order to properly satisfy and fulfill their technology needs. Provide refurbished and upgraded computers, computer equipment, computer labs and network wiring to schools, educational institutions and other charitable 501(c)(3) institutions dedicated to enhancing the learning opportunities of youth Educate students, underprivileged youth and their families as well as teachers through training in computer hardware knowledge and computer rebuilding as well as computer software training, including operating systems, application programs and website development. Properly recycling and/or donating to needy countries any computer or computer equipment that cannot be refurbished to reduce hazardous lead waste and other materials from filling their land fills Program / Activities (NTEE Code)

Student Services and Organizations

Computers for Youth (NY-based)

Train families on setting up and using computers.

Computers for Youth Foundation, Inc.

505 8th Ave

Ste 2402

New York, NY 10018

http://www.cfy.org

Mission and Programs

Mission

Across the nation, parents and policymakers are struggling with the problem of how to make their educational system work better, especially in low-income neighborhoods where high dropout rates are the norm. While most initiatives have focused on improving teachers' performance, little attention has been paid to improving students' motivation to learn. Computers for Youth (CFY) helps low-income students become engaged learners by using technology as a catalyst to improve their learning environment. They partner with public middle schools in poor neighborhoods and offer every family and teacher a home computer and their comprehensive services: training, email accounts, initial Internet access, ongoing technical support, and tailored web content at their Community Corner website. Almost all families and teachers participate; creating an effect that changes the learning environment. They help this change take root by offering the program to the incoming class each fall and thereby keeping their community saturated with technology. Their intervention purposefully catches students before they enter high school, where disengagement can result in their dropping out of school altogether. By using technology to engage middle-school students in their own learning, they enable them to succeed both in school and in life.

Programs

CFY provides inner-city students and their teachers with home computers and also provides schools with computers for use within the school building. Their programs include:

(1) Help Desk Program. CFY operates a professional help desk staffed by high school and college students. Their students get to develop marketable skills while providing

technical assistance, via phone and email, to the families and teachers who have received their computers.

(2) Training Program. CFY operates Saturday training sessions in the buildings of the schools they select. Students, parents and teachers must attend one half-day session before taking home their computer. New York Cares helps us recruit volunteer trainers for the sessions.

(3) Web Development Program. CFY has developed a website, www.communitycorner.org, for the families they serve so they have an inviting and easy-to-use entrance on to the Internet. CFY's commitment to having this website reflect their community's needs and interests has led them to develop their Web Development Internship Program. CFY hires and trains youth web development interns who represent the community they serve. These interns contribute to the conceptual and technical design of the site and create original content such as interviews with community leaders.

Program / Activities (NTEE Code)

Children's and Youth Services

Economic Development

Educational Services and Schools — Other

Results

Accomplishments for Fiscal Year ending 06/30/2004. Expanded their program by 15% from the prior year. Provided 1,500 inner-city students (and their families) and teachers with Pentium-level home computers and comprehensive services including training, Internet access, tech support, and web content. These recipients represent virtually all the students and teachers in six NYC public middle schools.

Expanded their training capacity to reach a record 120 families per Saturday (more than five times the number they reached per Saturday in their first year of operation).

Expanded their board of directors to 13 individuals.

Objectives for Fiscal Year Beginning 07/01/2004. Provide 1,500 inner city students and their teachers with

Pentium home computers and comprehensive services including training, Internet access, tech support and tailored web content. These recipients will represent all the incoming students at the six schools they worked with last year, as well as all the students and teachers in at least one additional middle school.

Continue to develop a growth strategy with the assistance of consultants from Monitor Company. Their current thinking is to expand CFY to three to four new cities within five years and to more than double their operations in NYC. This growth strategy will include developing an expanded revenue model to ensure they can sustain their growth over the long term.

Self-Assessment

CFY measures the effectiveness of its core program by assessing impact on three levels: (1) improved student engagement (students putting more effort into their education and feeling more confident as a result of having a home computer); (2) improved relationships that reinforce learning (students improving their relationships with family members and parents becoming more involved with their children's schooling (especially homework); and (3) better academic performance (students doing better in school and learning more as a result of having a home computer).

To measure these impacts, CFY uses a variety of instruments for research/evaluation, such as intake surveys, follow-up surveys, focus groups, interviews and an interval-contingent recording (ICR) technique or nightly log. This method is designed to reduce the problems of selective recall by asking young respondents to record their experiences on a nightly basis. Their research analysis includes statistical analysis of quantitative data and thematic coding of qualitative data derived from open-ended responses on the surveys, interviews, and nightly logs. To ensure the highest quality research, they work with consultants including individuals from the UCLA Psychology Department and Teachers College at Columbia University.

Chief Executive Profile

Ms. Stock began building CFY in 1999. Recognized as an expert in her field, Ms. Stock has served as an adviser to both the NYC Board of Education and the U.S. Department of Health and Human Services. She has been featured on National Public Radio and in the Wall Street Journal and has written a policy paper for the Benton Foundation. Prior to CFY, Ms. Stock served as a White House Fellow (1996-1997), where she was the principal architect of the Computers for Learning Program -- a program that enables Federal agencies to donate surplus computers directly to needy schools. She also worked at the Vera Institute of Justice and helped the Open Society Institute start up the After-School Corporation. She served for two years as a Peace Corps volunteer and later worked for the World Bank on appropriate technology in Africa, traveling extensively and publishing numerous articles. Ms. Stock served as a member of the MIT board of trustees (1997-2002) and is the youngest individual ever to be appointed as a member of the MIT Executive Committee (2000-2002). Crain's New York Business honored her in 2001 as one of 40 New Yorkers under 40 shaping the city. Ms. Stock is an MIT graduate with a bachelor's degree in engineering and master's degrees in urban planning, and technology and policy. She holds a patent for a medical device.

Additional Comments

CFY has been featured in the Wall Street Journal, National Public Radio, People Magazine and more. In only four years, they have distributed more than 3,000 computers and trained more than 6,000 students, parents and teachers in some of New York Cities poorest neighborhoods: East Harlem, the South Bronx, East New York, East Flatbush/Brownsville and Canarsie. CFY research has demonstrated that their program delivers significant impact on the three levels listed below: Improved student engagement

(1) More than 75% of CFY students said they put more effort into their education as a result of having a home

computer. Parents made comments such as: "He is more active in school and he earns extra credit on assignments", "She's more willing to do homework", and "He pays more attention at school".

(2) Almost 60% of teachers reported that using a home computer helped their students feel more confident. One parent stated that her daughter was "more confident of her knowledge of any given subject since she can research it on the computer".

Relationships that reinforce learning

(1) 71% of the parents told us that they used their home computers to help their children with homework. Specific examples they gave included practicing writing essays using certain words and helping research information for a science fair project.

(2) 57% of parents indicated that access to a home computer had improved their children's relationships with family members: kids became closer to one another by playing games together and became closer with parents by

teaching them new computer skills and showing them their work.

Better academic performance

(1) 74% of CFY students said that having a home computer helped them do better in school. Anecdotes from parents help illustrate this point. For example, one parent commented that his son had done better in science and math; he's gone from a grade "C" to a "B". Another parent noted that in social studies, his son "got a B+ rather then his usual Cs and Ds".

(2) 58% of CFY students said they learn more in school as a result of having a home computer.

Technology Recycling Program

Donate Your Computer

Find out how you can bridge the digital divide by donating your old computer equipment.

Computers for All

Donations of new and used computers, parts, and hardware Computers for Youth

Corporate donations of 50 or more computers at a time

Lazarus Foundation

Nonprofit computer recycling foundation

Computer recycling for education

National Cristina Foundation

Donate computers to help children with special needs

Hub Heaven, Inc.

888 Seventh Ave

18th Fl

New York, NY 10106

http://www.heavens.org

Mission and Programs

Mission

HEAVEN -- Helping Educate, Activate, Volunteer & Empower via the Net -- is a 501(c)(3) national nonprofit organization and website.

Their mission is twofold: to provide an online forum for positive social change; and to get under served youth the tools and training they need to succeed.

By bringing together charitable causes and volunteer opportunities, HEAVEN helps you find out where, when, how and why you can make a difference. Through their ANGELS computer training career development and community service program, HEAVEN uses the Internet as a democratizing force to narrow the digital divide.

Visit HEAVEN at heavens.org or keyword: heaven on AOL.

Programs

In HEAVEN:

* HEAVENLY BODIES (personalities and supermodels who are above all role models) welcome you in, shedding light on causes they care about and how you can get involved.

* GOOD COMPANY profiles companies and organizations that effect change --- from Timberland's "Give Racism the Boot" campaign to Surfrider's mandate to keep our oceans clean.

* VOLUNTEER NOW! Connects you with volunteer opportunities in your neck of the woods and areas of interest, matching millions of people with organizations that need their time, talent, goods, services and skills.

* CLOUD NINE/ISSUES features issue-oriented articles and essays by leading writers, activists and artists; and encourages you to join the debate, share solutions and create a community dedicated to social change.

* HALO EFFECT offers up members' own accounts of ordinary and extraordinary differences made daily.

ANGELS (America's Network of Givers, Educators, Learners and Servers), a real-world computer training and community service program for inner-city high school students, brings it all home --- establishing a nationwide effort to ensure that young people have access to the computer skills, technology, job opportunities and mentors they deserve.

*DIGITAL DIVIDE Recently, HEAVEN released its "Guide to the Digital Divide" to address the who, what and why of the Digital Divide and offer practical ways all of us can make a difference.

Program / Activities (NTEE Code)

Philanthropy/Charity/Voluntarism Promotion (General) Other Youth Development N.E.C.

Results

Accomplishments for Fiscal Year ending 12/01/1998. Graduated a total of 75 students from the ANGELS program.

Received ComputerWorld/Smithsonian Award from the Smithsonian Museum.

Re-designed Web site.

Objectives for Fiscal Year Beginning 01/01/1999 were: Expand the ANGELS program to serve more communities.

Make HEAVEN's site a popular destination for things charitable.

Create an After-School Activist Center.

Chief Executive Profile

With extensive experience in community organizing and marketing, Wendy Dubit has been the primary force behind several successful start-ups, among them: Wine Enthusiast Magazine, WorldWise Marketing, Jim Henson Records, CD-MOM: The Family Place in Cyberspace, OutHouse Productions, Urban Legends, and FarmHands-CityHands -- - a groundbreaking non-profit whose efforts to link farm and city have served as the model for subsequent public and private initiatives at home and abroad.

Additional Comments

HEAVEN has been awarded several honors in its short year and a half of existence. The Smithsonian Museum has awarded HEAVEN a ComputerWorld/Smithsonian Award honoring its visionary uses of technology. HEAVEN's ANGELS computer training, career development and community service program has been adopted and largely funded by the New York City Board of Education, and awaits replications in Detroit, Chicago and Los Angeles.

There are also a large number of computer technology recycling programs that are associated with the above-mentioned charitable organizations.

African and African American males are helped by the above programs however if all of the charitable organizations mentioned above would focus all of their resources to the minority group most negatively effected by the Digital Divide, the African and African American male, they could resolve the Digital Divide tragedy for him and then could move on to the next group in need of priorital assistance.   Much more is learned and much more efficiency achieved by dealing with issues under a microscope rather then just throwing limited valuable resources into many different areas only effecting the problem in a small way.

Focus by public and government resources and programs are also being implemented and under development and the next chapter discusses the importance of these assets and how they should be directed and primarily how you as a citizen in whatever country you may be can get involved in government by introducing the African and African American male Digital Divide issue to your government bodies.

Chapter 7

Why African and African American Females?

Studies have revealed that African and African American women are making great strides in decreasing the gap between their selves and white people regarding the Digital Divide. There is much evidence that the African American female will be statistically equal to White people within the very next few years in some areas. This means the female African and African American is making progress unlike the male whose statistics are flat. For example, the percentage of women owning PCs at home has increased over time for White women, but not as much as African American women however not to as great an extent as the difference between White males and African American males and also African American women were much more likely than White women to be new users, but over time this difference has disappeared showing that the African American woman has become equal with White women and the Digital Divide no longer exists amongst them in this particular area.

African and African American women are making progress while the African and African American men are falling behind. Fundamentally this is wrong. The African and African American male has need for technology as much as all others need technology. Immediate assistance must be made available to him to allow him access to technology and training so that he may use the technology well. The African and African American female must continue striving to bridge the gaps in technology that still exist in her world. The African and African American females on average have a better understanding of more difficult subject areas taught in primary and secondary schools. Improvement in this area by African and African males would increase the number of African and African American males accepted into good colleges and decrease the number of high school college dropouts.

Chapter 8

Public Intervention for the African and African American Male Digital Divide-How to Write A Bill

Educators around the world are continuously attempting to solve the social and economic problems that are faced by society. There resources are limited by small budgets and limited manpower, however educators have recognized the problems related to being an African or African American male and are attempting to institute new policies that target the African and African American males sui generis problems that block him from succeeding in school and in real-life.

Teachers are trying to be more lenient toward the African and African American male to reduce the amount of suspensions and dismissals from schools and are attempting to lower the bar on the African and African American males' acceptance into gifted programs and are attempting to improve the recruitment and training of teachers in the schools that primarily serve the African and African American community (Gibbs, 1988; Reed, 1988).

Public sponsored private tutoring programs designed for specific needs of African and African American males must be sponsored and also public sponsoring of African and African American males in quality private primary and secondary schools would help the African and African American male dominate scholastically and thereby provide him with an open door to a high quality private higher institutions of learning, thusly, decreasing their plight throughout. Government and social programs alone cannot solve the social and economic problems in the U.S. that so severely limit opportunities of African American males. Nonetheless, many educators and other concerned citizens are introducing new practices targeted specifically to their unique needs. Efforts are also being made to decrease the suspension and expulsion rates of African American males, to lower their representation in general tracks and special education programs and raise it in programs for the gifted and talented, and to improve the recruitment and training of teachers and counselors in predominantly African and African American schools (Gibbs, 1988; Reed, 1988).

Government policy can also be changed and the constitutions of governments' can be modified to address the African and African American Digital Divide Issue. The following is an example of what I thought an African and African American Digital Divide Bill should look like. This bill would work well in the United States, however it could be easily modified to suit any country.

"The African American Digital Divide Bill-African American Males Without Technology"

Africans and African American's have been victims of diversity throughout history. There are countless instances of inequality that are well documented throughout American history, yet in this study I have determined that the African American, in particular the African American male, is still the victim of another inequality, the Digital Divide, and since they are victim of such diversity, why should the life of an African American male be one without access to technology. They have already looked at how this occurs and therefore they will continue with both my opinion and proven methodologies that will help us to see what we as United States citizens can do to help the African American male reach equilibrium within the remainder of the population. African American females have already made amazing improvement in decreasing the Digital Divide for their gender and therefore I assert that we citizens of the United States must work to help the African

American males in decreasing the Digital Divide for themselves.

Negative Effects of Life Without Technology

There are many effects of life without technology. For one, the use of a computer on the Internet and the amount one reveals about his or herself is controlled by the user of the technology. For instance, studies have proven that students of other then white ethnic origin often perform better while taking distance learning program classes and that the more anonymous students of other then ethnic origin are the better they perform on their coursework over when they are utilizing a traditional classroom. In my opinion it is because their teachers and fellow students have no way of knowing what they look like, if they are African American or Chinese-American and many times even if they are male or female. A recent study published in the online edition of "Nature Neuroscience" determined through the use of brain imaging (fMRI), which measures brain activity, that when people of White ethnicity are in the presence of African American people that problem solving skills diminish within the White individual. The reason for the diminished mental resources was determined to be due to the White individuals suppression of racial bias. The suppression of racial bias apparently exhausts mental resources. A synopsis of the Dartmouth study is available at: http://www.dartmouth.edu/~news/releases/2003/11/17.html in the Dartmouth News.

It is has not yet been assessed whether the same diminishment of mental capacity occurs when African Americans are exposed to White people and there are many other interesting artifacts to collect from this type of study including as to whether distance learning over the Internet would produce the same results in a controlled laboratory experiment rather than only statistically. There being no face to face interaction in most distance learning courses, these types of studies point to conclusions that African American males improve there learning experiences with distance learning technology and if this is the case then here is another reason why the African American male is a victim of digital diversity that can be improved by providing him with adequate resources.

A poll by National Public Radio, the Kaiser Family Foundation, and Harvard's Kennedy School of Government has found that the majority of Americans feel that computers and the Internet have made Americans' lives better. This study relates to many citations on how White-Americans in the upper income ranges have overwhelmingly rich access to the Internet and computer technology and the racial differences regarding who gets access to technology is disgraceful. Digital discrimination in homes is rampant. Internet access is hugely divided by race in the homes of America. The resources of African American males are lacking in many areas of American society primarily due to not having the same opportunities of other Americans. No access to the Internet or computer technology puts them at a distinct disadvantage. In order to better themselves people need to be competitive with technology. At first glance, not having a PC in ones home seems trivial and non-consequential, however the financial rewards of technology are many. The ability to perform computer aided functions such as writing a neat resume with a PC software program, doing a simple search for employment over the Internet, the ability to pursue academic goals through online coursework, access to financial information and e-mail and fax capabilities shows that the African American male is at a comparative disadvantage as to those who have access. There is a gap of 11 percentage points between African Americans and white Americans using computers at work, but there is even a larger gap, 22 percentage points, between African Americans (52%) and White Americans (73%) who have a computer at home and a similar gap is prevalent in terms of Internet access as well. While African American kids (44%) are considerably less likely to use a computer at home than White American kids (76%).

Who uses computers?

Percent of Difference	=21Percent
White Americans w' Computer at Home	=73Percent
African American w' Computer at Home	=52Percent
Percent of Difference	=32Percent
White American Kids w' Computer at Home	=44Percent
African American Kids w' Computer at Home	=76Percent

Here is a brief summary of facts that conclude that the African American is unequally impeded when it comes to access and use of technology.

-90.2 percent of private college freshman use the Internet for research, yet only 77.6 percent of students entering public African American colleges report doing so. (Sax, Astin, Korn, & Mahoney, 1998).

-80.1 percent of private college freshman use email regularly, only 41.4 percent of students attending African American public colleges do. (Sax, Astin, Korn, & Mahoney, 1998).

-70 percent of the schools in this country have at least one computer connected to the Internet, less than 15 percent of classrooms have Internet access (Harmon, 1997).

-Although numerous studies (CyberAtlas, 1999; Maraganore & Morrisette, 1998) suggest that the gender gap in Internet use appears to be closing over time and that Internet users are increasingly coming from the ranks of those with lower education and income (Pew Research Center, 1998), the perception persists that the gap for race is not decreasing (Abrams, 1997).

Who is able to do research with the Internet?

Private Freshman Internet Research	90.20%
Public African and African American Freshman Internet Research	77.60%
Private College Freshman Email Use	80.10%
Public African and African American Freshman Email Use	41.40%
Schools with Computers	70.00%
Schools with Internet Access	15.00%

A study on racial differences done by Hoffman and Novak (1998) found that Whites were significantly more likely to have a computer in their home as well as at work. In addition, the research concluded that Whites were less likely to have ever used the Web at home, whereas African Americans were slightly more likely to have ever used the

Web at school. It was also determined in this study that Whites were still more likely to own a home computer than were African Americans and to have used the Web recently, despite differences in education. The study also concluded that the Digital Divide for Web usage was equal when a computer was present in both the African Americans and the White households. However, it was determined that White people have more resources available to them to gain access to the Web then do African Americans and therefore the Whites were more likely to have accessed the Web then the African Americans.

Another research study done by the Commerce Department's National Telecommunications and Information Administration (McConnaughey & Lader, 1998) analyzed data on computer penetration rates from the October 1997 Census Current Population Survey as part of an ongoing examination of the digital divide. The study came to the conclusion that between the November 1994 CPS and the one in 1998, the Commerce Department's

National   Telecommunications   and   Information
Administration (McConnaughey & Lader, 1998) analyzed
data on computer penetration rates from the October 1997
Census Current Population Survey (CPS) as part of an
ongoing examination of the digital divide. This analysis
represented an update from their 1995 study of similar
data from the November 1994 Census Current Population
Survey and they concluded that between 1994 and 1997
the gap between African Americans and Whites was
actually greater when considering home computer
ownership and Internet access. African American
households rose from 11.2% to 23.5% since December
1998 in a CPS study. This compares to an overall rise in
Internet access by U.S. Households over the same period
from 26.2% to 41.5% (or 43.6 million households).

United States policy is thought to be one of the
contributing factors to the growing Digital Divide between
African American and White people (Cooper and
Kimmelman 1999). It is suspected that U.S. Policy has

decreased the level of competition between the telecommunications and cable industries thusly making access to the Internet more expensive then it should be.

In a graduate report at a Vanderbilt University Study called "The Evolution of the Digital Divide-How Gaps in Internet Access May Impact Electronic Commerce" by Donna L. Hoffman, Thomas P. Novak, Ann E. Schlosser, it was surveyed that the relationship between gender and Web access and use for Whites and African Americans that Web access and use are lower for women than men and that among recent Web users, men are more likely to have been using the Web longer, and to have used the Web more recently and that women are more likely to be newer users. The interesting data collected in this study is that while White men are more frequent Web users than White women, African American men are not more frequent Web users than African American women. What follows is an analysis of differences by race for each gender.

The study shows that in the Men category, White men consistently are more likely to have access to the Web as well as to have ever used the Web and to have owned a PC at home more than African American men and that these differences have continued over time. White men owning a PC at home has grown for White men, yet not for the African American male. White men are slightly more likely to have PC access at work as well.

Among recent Web users, African American men are much more likely than White men to be newer Web users and this finding persists over time. White men were more than three times as likely as African American men to have been online for two years or more (20.31 percent versus 6.20 percent), where fifty percent of White and African American men had been online that long.

Percentage of New Web Using: White Males vs. New African and African American males.

White Males	African and African American Male
6.20 Percent	20.31 Percent

According to the report White Males were more likely to be the most recent Web users than African American men at a percentage rate of 65.46 for White Males as compared to 37.04 percent for the African American Male.

Percentage of More Recent Web Usage: White Males vs. African and African American males

White Males	African and African American Male
65.46 Percent	37.04 Percent

White men were also more frequent Web users than African American men at a rate of 55.94 percent versus 38.9 percent even though later studies have showed an increase by both White Males and African American males.

Percentage of More Frequent Web Usage: White Males vs. New African and African American males.

White Males	African and African American Male
55.94 Percent	38.9 Percent

The study asserts that over time, the percentage of African American men ever using the Web at home, work, school or other locations has increased considerably and that the percentage of White males who ever used the Web at school is flat, has grown only in small amounts for home and work, and has fallen for ever used at other locations. African American men were more likely to have ever used the Web at school or at other locations, compared to White men.

Change in Web useage.

| African and African Americans Ever Using the Web at Home, School, or Other Locations Increased |
| The Percentage of White Males Who Ever Used the Web at School is Flat |

Also this same study concluded that White women are more likely than African American women to have access to the Web as well as to have ever used the Web, to own a PC and to have PC access at work and these differences have persisted over time. As for men, the percentage of women owning PCs at home has increased over time for White women, but not African American women, however not to as great an extent as the difference between White Males and African American males and also African American women were much more likely than White women to be new users, but over time this difference has disappeared showing that the African American woman has become equal with White women and the Digital Divide no longer exists amongst them in this particular area.

Consequences

The Digital Divide between the African American Male and the White Male has significant negative consequences to the United States (Beaupre & Brand-Williams, 1997). The lack of computer skills within the African American males could be disastrous as the demand for computer-trained employees grows. These men are needed in America's workforce to keep our businesses competitive with foreign competition. In addition, there is consideration regarding the freedom of expression that is available to those people who have access to the Internet. Also, consider that since there is such a large deficit between African American males and White American Males in home PC and Internet access at this present time, the opportunities lost by the African Americans as compared to the White Americans are devastating. Think of what it was like for the African American male when he wasn't allowed to own his own business or work at his own job or own his own land and then look at the huge difference it made in the quality of life and in contrast to the advances made by the White American Male whom having all of these freedoms given to him excelled while the African American Male to this day has to wait in line before he can reap the rewards of a high speed Internet connection. This disparity has denigrated and continues to denigrate the African American male and it will continue to denigrate them for generations to come if something isn't done now to end their prolonged suffering due to their digital disparity.

What Can Citizens Do to Narrow the Divide?

As a citizen, there are many things that must be done to decrease the digital divide between African American males and White males. For example, when possible make certain that we arrange access to the computer systems at schools with access hours for exclusive use of the systems for

African American male students. In addition, it is possible to have school administrators start a sharing program where students with computer access at home are asked to help African American male students by inviting them into their homes and allowing them to use their computer systems. It is possible for teachers, administrators, and students alike to ask government officials to do something about the Digital Divide issue between African Americans males and White males. As a suggestion they could publicly and privately sponsor tech shops where African American males can go to gain Internet access and increase Web accessibility in public and private libraries and other government and privately owned buildings for the African American male. United States citizens have the right to draft legislation that can be submitted to the United States Congress. Also, large computer companies should be encouraged by the government to offer discounted rates to African American males and also provide them with tutoring to show them how to use the technology to their advantage in society.

Changing or improving current government policy involving the African American male is a difficult issue; yet changing government policy is the most powerful tool the United States can afford to a group being discriminated against. The following are some government policy changes that should be added to our constitution regarding changing and improving government policy to help resolve the African American male Digital Divide crisis: The Legislature of the World

SB / HB # _____ (this number is assigned by the clerk)

SPONSORED BY: _____

REFERRED TO: _____ (committee referrals are made by the presiding officer) RELATES TO: The Digital Divide

TITLED The African and African American males Without Technology Act

-Policy 1: All African and African American males have the right to utilize all public personal computers that are available to the general public on a priority basis and are encouraged by law to use these rights and all other citizens are forbidden to discriminate against the African and African American male by law and violators are punishable by law.

-Policy 2: All African and African American males are entitled to government grants for the purchase of a personal computer and Internet service and have the right to utilize such entitlements and eligibility without suffering from prejudice or discriminatory practices which are punishable by law.

-Policy 3: All African and African American males are entitled and eligible for government funded training on the use of personal computers and Internet usage and have the right to utilize such entitlements and eligibility and all citizens are forbidden to discriminate against him while he is utilizing these benefits.

-Policy 4: All African American males will be notified of their rights and benefits available by law and shall not be subject to prejudice due to the preferences provided by this bill and any prejudice or interference will be punishable by law.

This bill is meant to resolve the African and African American male Digital Divide as a problem that is getting worse rather than better and more attention must be spent on this problem to get it under control. The Digital Divide can make a difference as to whether an African and or an African American male will do well in school as opposed to dropping out or just barely getting by. There is a study regarding the effect of education on crime and Incarceration by Lance Lochner and Enrico Moretti, in their JCPR working paper, "The Effect of Education on Crime." Their research concluded that between 1960-1980, incarceration rates for White men with less than 12 years of schooling averaged roughly 0.8%, and for African American men, they averaged 3.6%. I understand that this study is a little outdated, yet if an African American having access to the Internet increases there chances of them doing better scholastically then it would be a good idea to provide this to them for societies sake. The authors' of the study mentioned above have found a significant effect of education on incarceration and crime, with the impact greater for African Americans. On average, one additional year of school results in a 0.1 percentage point reduction in the probability of incarceration for Whites, and a 0.4 percentage point reduction for African Americans.

To put this in context, differences in average education between African Americans and Whites can explain as much as 23% of the African American/White gap in incarceration rates. Therefore, to provide Internet access will provide more learning opportunities to African Americans and in conclusion will therefore help society in a great way and greatly improvise the African American males learning experience when they participate in distance learning through the Internet with a personal computer. If

Congress would pass legislation to supply Internet access and personal computers' to African American males this legislation would have a significantly positive effect on the African American male. Below are some statistics related to the African American/White gap in incarceration rates.

Incarceration rates:

White 12 yrs. School or less	.8%
African American 12 yrs. School or less	3.60%
Percentage Difference	2.80%

Also, the African American male achieves more in a Distance Learning Environment where all of their course work is completed over the Internet and face-to-face confrontation with teachers and other students is not necessary. This study found that African American males did achieve more in this environment, and therefore we should provide funding to programs to provide them with the essential tools they need to achieve in the world of academia and life. Avoidance of interracial interactions and there negative side effects can be masked through the use of the Internet and through distance learning tools, and therefore they should be provided the advantages they need to overcome the prejudicial treatment.

I do hereby submit this bill to be voted into Law.

The above was an example of what a Bill to help save the African and African American male from his plight regarding the Digital Divide should be inclusive of. If a Bill such as this were passed in every country throughout the world it would create a multitude of benefits to the entire population of our planet.

Chapter 9

Private Intervention: Privately Sponsored Programs'

Private intervention includes both corporate and private sponsorship. There are many companies attempting to bridge the gap and below are listed many programs sponsored by corporations.

AOL/Time Warner Foundation: AOLTWF supports programs that use the Internet to improve the lives of families, children and the disadvantaged. Their program is focused on the theme 'Skills for Success for the Next Generation'. It is wonderful that they have brought there Internet savvy and financial muscle to tackle the Digital

Divide issue and their heart is in the right place, however, they should be focusing on groups where the need for their support is greatest, the African and African-American male, and the time to focus on this group is now, not in the next generation.

AOLTWF has a mission statement that is worded as follows: Time Warner is committed to serving the public interest through the philanthropic and volunteer efforts of the company and its employees. We are focused on developing the next generation of leaders from among diverse and under served youth by helping them acquire the skills and competencies they need to succeed.

We do this by:

Engaging young people in the creative and media arts, increasing the opportunities for under served teens to prepare for college, and fostering leadership in the public schools.

We primarily invest in after school or other youth programs, which involve hands-on learning, leadership development, decision-making opportunities and skill building.

The Foundation makes grants to:

National and community-based after-school organizations which engage creative and media arts and prepare under served teens for college and are involved in organizations that work to raise awareness of the need for quality after-school programs.

Efforts to foster leadership opportunities for public school students in selected cities.

The following community-based organizations were recently selected to receive two-year grants through the Time Warner Grants program.

911 Media Arts Center (Seattle, WA)

Appalshop (Whitesburg, KY)

Bay Area Video Coalition (San Francisco, CA)

Downtown Community Television (New York, NY) Educational Video Center (New York, NY)

Global Action Project (New York, NY)

Global Kids (New York, NY)

Plugged In (East Palo Alto, CA)

Southwest Youth Collaborative (Chicago, IL)

Spy Hop Productions (Salt Lake City, UT)

Video Machete (Chicago, IL)

WNYC Radio Rookies (New York, NY)

Youth Communication (New York, NY)

Youth Radio (Berkeley, CA).

AT&T Foundation: This Foundation invests in education, civic and community service, and the arts in communities where AT&T has a significant business presence. AT&T with all of their resources could easily end the suffering of the African and African American male if the company would focus its resources on them specifically. Again, they should be focusing on the groups that need their support the most and carry on group by group. This company provides a lot of general assistance and is not primarily focused on the problems created by the Digital Divide, however they do participate in international online learning programs that sometimes focus attention on the problems faced by the African and African American male regarding the Digital Divide.

Below is a description of one of the pieces of their efforts to provide online educational resources to students throughout the world: The GVF program consists of a cadre of distinguished scholars and practitioners from around the world who serve as Global Virtual Faculty members in partnership with the on-campus faculty in teaching of our on-line courses. As every undergraduate is required to enroll in one Internet-based distance-learning course for each year of study, it was only natural to bring together the distance learning requirement and their commitment to global education by engaging Global Virtual Faculty. The primary role of a GVF member is to bring a global dimension to the learning experience by offering different perspectives and observations to students on the issues under study.

BellSouth Foundation: This Foundation funds education reform activities in the Southeast that will have an impact on a substantial number of students in school systems or post-secondary institutions, or across communities, states or regions. This program focuses much on United States southern schools with a large amount of African American male students and appears to benefit many, again however, if their full resources were focused on the African and African American male Digital Divide issue the problem would be resolved quickly. Below is a description of their program: The BellSouth Foundation invests the majority of its grant making funds in its Special Initiatives through a targeted request for proposal process. However, a limited number of Opportunity Grants are available for unsolicited proposals that compliment Special Initiatives or issues where the BellSouth Foundation is currently focusing its work.

In general (and as funds permit), Opportunity Grants will be awarded to programs or projects that: Mesh tightly with one of the Foundation's strategies; (Their current grant making Special Initiatives include College-Going Minorities, Leadership, Quality in the Classroom, Proniño, and Power to Learn. In addition, the BellSouth Foundation awards a limited number of Opportunity Grants—or responses to unsolicited proposals).

Offer a complementary strategy for the Foundation's other work; Offer a new and innovative approach to a priority issue; provide a supportive policy-level effort to supplement a Foundation priority; or Serve as a collaborative practice for a Foundation initiative.

Issues of new interest in 2004 evolving from past years efforts are: Technology & Learning: One of the unique findings within the BellSouth edu.pwr3 technology initiative is that students' view of technology in learning is different from the view of schools. Grants in this area will be awarded to support further exploration of incorporating 'student voice' to build meaningful use of technology for learning for students. View BellSouth Big Difference report to see some of the latest work of the BellSouth Foundation in this area.

No Child Left Behind: The national No Child Left Behind (NCLB) legislation requires that school districts invest dollars, attention and energy into several factors targeted toward improving student achievement. Grants in this area will be awarded to districts seeking support to fulfill requirements of NCLB— especially with respect to addressing the "Stronger Accountability" standards outlined in NCLB. For more information on NCLB in your state visit: http://nclb.ecs.org/nclb/ Business/Education Partnerships: Partnerships between the education community and local businesses show great promise for sustained positive change and broader community involvement and support in local schools and school districts. The Foundation is interested in helping to strengthen existing partnerships between school districts and local businesses, and in helping to foster new partnerships for change that promise lasting results. Cisco

Foundation: This Foundation provides funds for community projects in San Jose, California, with a focus on education, workforce development and basic human needs. Here though is a high-tech company that could easily end the African and African American Digital Divide issue on their own if they focused on the problem. Here is more specific information on the program: Cisco Impact Philanthropy is about building strong and productive global communities in which every individual has the means to live, the opportunity to learn, and the chance to give back. Any one of these essentials is enough to make a difference in the present, but it takes all three to set in motion an enduring cycle of health and prosperity.

Its goal is to identify nonprofits that do outstanding work in one or more segments of the cycle, as shown at right. Supported are organizations and communities in immediate distress, and they help expand their long-term capacity by encouraging the innovative integration of technology into their operational strategies.

The result? Nonprofits reach new levels of productivity, and chronic intervention steadily gives way to lasting transformation. That's what sets their philanthropy apart. That's the Cisco Impact.

IBM Philanthropy Grants and Fund for Community Service: The majority of these grants focus on K-12 education initiatives with some smaller grants for economic workforce development and arts and culture. With the technical and financial capacity of this mighty corporation the African and African American male Digital Divide issue would be made extinct within 30 days if IBM applied it's full charitable resource capabilities to the issue. Here is what IBM's current philanthropic focus is: IBM's central commitment is education:

IBM counts education as the top priority in its philanthropic efforts. Through Reinventing Education and other strategic efforts, we're solving education's toughest problems with solutions that draw on advanced information technologies and the best minds IBM can apply. Their programs pave the way for systematic reform in school systems nationwide through partnerships with whole school districts and entire states.

A commitment to corporate citizenship

"Good Philanthropy is Good Business..."

IBM corporate philanthropy spans the globe with diverse and sustained programs that support initiatives in education, workforce development and arts and culture to benefit communities in need. IBM provides grant recipients with technology, project funds, and employee time and talent. IBM's On Demand Community is a first-of-its kind initiative to encourage and sustain corporate philanthropy through employee volunteerism. To learn more about the social, economic and environmental dimensions of their business activities, products and services, please read their first Corporate Responsibility Report.

News and highlights

IBM launches first worldwide volunteer initiative aimed at company retirees. IBM announced the next step in its On

Demand Community volunteer initiative by enabling its approximately 160,000 retirees to leverage new technology tools to increase the impact and value of volunteer efforts in schools and local agencies across the globe.

IBM Mexico Ranked Number One in Corporate Reputation. IBM Mexico has been named the company with the best corporate reputation in the sector of Information and Telecommunications in a recent index compiled by the not-for-profit group, Mexican Transparency, and Consulta Mitofsky, a public opinion agency.

Independent evaluation identifies Reinventing Education as a model for school reform. According to a new study issued by the Center for Children and Technology, IBM's grant initiative is driving higher achievement in classrooms and re-writing the rules for successful school-business partnerships.

Chinese Ministry of Education and IBM Launch Reinventing Education Partnership. China became the 11th country to receive an IBM Reinventing Education grant. The partnership supports basic education reforms focusing on the development of new curriculum and teaching methodologies.

IBM and the Egyptian government provide access to Egypt's cultural heritage. An extraordinary partnership between the Egyptian government and IBM has created "Eternal Egypt" providing worldwide access to 7,000 years of Egyptian history. The project combines the most important locations, artifacts, people and stories from Egypt's history into an interactive multimedia experience.

IBM Launches On Demand Community Volunteer Initiative. On November 15, 2003, IBM introduced a first-of-its kind initiative to encourage and sustain corporate philanthropy through volunteerism by arming employees with a rich set of IBM technology tools targeted for non-profit community organizations and schools.

IBM Australia receives high marks in corporate social responsibility rating. IBM Australia is number two in a ranking of the Top 100 companies for social responsibility in that country, according to a Reputex survey released on October 13, 2003.

IBM launches ¡TradúceloAhora! Automatic Translation Project across the United States. Hispanics with access to English content on the World Wide Web will soon have access to richer, higher quality information through a new initiative announced today by IBM.

Virtual Counselor is the latest service from the Broward County/IBM Reinventing Education partnership. By providing secure, real-time information to parents and students, the Virtual Counselor is the newest example of how Reinventing Education is supporting families and public schools.

IBM MentorPlace unveils new online tool for Fall 2003. IBM has teamed with EdReach, Inc. to develop a secure online communications tool for IBM MentorPlace. The tool is being used to register an anticipated 8,000 IBM volunteers in more than 15 countries.

First European Early Learning conference confirms strong role for ICT in expanding early childhood education. Participants at the first European conference on ICT in early learning, organized by IBM in Brussels on May 22nd and 23rd, recommended that education ministries review teacher training strategies so that all pre-school teachers are trained to integrate ICT effectively into early education settings.

The State Hermitage Museum and IBM announce the Hermitage Virtual Academy. IBM and the State Hermitage Museum of St. Petersburg, Russia announced the launch of the Hermitage Virtual Academy, a collection of dynamic web-based courses available to the general public.

IBM receives 2002 Award for Excellence in Corporate Community Service. IBM has been honored with the 2002 Award for Excellence in Corporate Community Service from the Points of Light Foundation. IBM was among a handful of companies that were recognized for successfully integrating employee volunteer programs into their core business operations and creating supportive environments that inspire and enable employees to volunteer in the communities in which they live and work. According to Points of Light, IBM Corporation's overall employee volunteer efforts and the program policies and corporate vision that support those volunteer activities are true examples of corporate volunteerism at its best.

MarcoPolo: This collaboration of MCIWorldCom and major education institutions, provides innovative standards-based curricula to teachers. They also support a grant program targeted at school districts. This program is funded by several corporate giants and has very good intentions yet the primary focus should be on the African and African American male Digital Divide. Here is more information on this program: The MarcoPolo Education Foundation (MPEd) was launched by the MCI Foundation in 2002, to broaden the base of support for the MarcoPolo program. MPEd strives to meet the needs of teachers and students through the ongoing development and delivery of a broad base of educational technology products and services for cost recovery, including high-quality professional development training and materials. Grants from the public and private sector allow MPEd to provide targeted and customized professional development programs in select school districts and region. Since the program's inception in 1997, MCI has provided over $49 million in funding for MarcoPolo, in addition to its in kind contributions of staff, infrastructure, and management. MarcoPolo is an important part of MCI's commitment to improving our nation's education system by leveraging the Internet to improve teaching and learning through free, high-quality Internet content and extensive training for teachers for integrating the Internet into the classroom.

Microsoft has provided $200,000 in funding to the MarcoPolo Education Foundation to accelerate the development of additional interactive student resources. The funding will help MarcoPolo Content Partners more quickly meet teacher demand for interactive materials to use with their students. Embedded within MarcoPolo Content Partner lessons, these Flash-based tools allow students to manipulate, experiment, and interact with Marco Polo's online educational content in innovative and exciting ways that appeal to technology-savvy students. Examples of interactives that will be built with this funding include flash cards, mapping and vocabulary tools. In addition, Microsoft will link to MarcoPolo content into Microsoft's Innovative Teachers program.

The GE Foundation, the philanthropic foundation of the General Electric Company, is providing $250,000 in funding to the National Council of Teachers of Mathematics (NCTM), in partnership with the MarcoPolo consortium, to lead an initiative to help close the Digital Divide and achievement gap in mathematics. The funding is being used to develop online Mathematics content and interactives and deliver training to hundreds of teachers in under served schools within select GE communities.

Microsoft Giving: Microsoft Giving is focused on creating greater access to information technology in disadvantaged communities worldwide. This is accomplished through the support of higher education, youth programs, nonprofit technology solutions, public libraries and the creative community.   The African and African American male is waiting for this giant to give them a hand. If the resources were focused the problem would be solved. Here is what the MicroSoft Giving program does: Microsoft's 20-year history of community engagement has fostered a variety of key community partnerships built on the mutual commitment to find sustainable technology solutions that make real and lasting differences in people's lives. Again, the African and African American male aid should come first.

Microsoft® Unlimited Potential (UP) is the primary focus of Microsoft's corporate philanthropy efforts. UP is a global program focused on partnering with others to provide technology skills for under served young people and adults through community-based technology and learning centers (CTLCs).

Ultimately, Microsoft believes that by providing training and tools, we can partner to create social and economic opportunities that can transform communities and help people realize their potential. Last year alone, Microsoft contributed more than US$40 million in cash and US$224 million in software to nearly 5,000 nonprofit organizations.

I would like to take a moment to again besiege these corporate giants to think of the issues of the African and African American male and the Digital Divide as their number one concern. These people have waited long enough. As each year goes by approximately another million African and African American male children and adults' lives are ruined by forces beyond their control and much of the destruction could be avoided with training in technology and access to computer and Internet resources in their homes and schools and in public and private areas.

Private Funding

This section is about the private funding available for those in need and again if any one of these funds were focused directly at the African and African American male Digital Divide issue there would be a problem any longer. Here is a list of private funding institutions and foundations: Since 1948, the Annie E. Casey Foundation (AECF) has worked to build better futures for disadvantaged children and their families in the United States. The primary mission of the Foundation is to foster public policies, human service reforms, and community supports that more effectively meet the needs of today's vulnerable children and families. Here is what this Foundation does and again the African and African American Digital Divide issue would become extinct if this foundation decided to do so.

Annie E. Casey Foundation's policy magazine. The Spring 2004 issue explores the workforce crisis plaguing children and family services. AECF President Doug Nelson highlights the need for renewed focus on front line workers serving needy kids and families, and we look up-close at this challenge in Greenville, South Carolina. Other articles document Michigan's "just-in-time" hiring process and Cincinnati's pay-for-performance contract with area human services workers. A final article profiles three more promising personnel reforms.

The Casey Foundation is a major supporter of the Reentry National Media Outreach Campaign, which showcases communication resources focusing on the reintegration of the 600,000 men and women leaving prison annually and returning to their families and communities. The website provides discussion guides, clips from TV and radio productions, and "Outside the Walls: A National Snapshot of Community-Based Prisoner Reentry Programs." 1/27/04 Latest data on child well being now available! Their 15th annual KIDS COUNT Data Book provides a state-by-state statistical portrait of the educational, health, and economic conditions of American children. This year's essay focuses on the increasing number of "disconnected" youth without degrees or employment who face a tough transition to adulthood. Order the Data Book and related products; create customized data reports, and more. Read President Doug Nelson's remarks at the Youth Summit.

The Right Start For America's Newborns: City and State Trends 1990-2001, a KIDS COUNT online report, addresses the Foundation's belief that conditions under which infants are born can have lifelong effects on child development and school readiness. The report uses data from birth certificates to track key measures of child well-being in the 50 states and 55 large cities in the US. Read the report or view profiles, graphs, maps, rankings, and more.

1/29/04 KIDS COUNT: State-Level Measures of Child Well-Being for Children of Color provide statistics on economic, educational, and social well-being for children of color in the US from the 2000 Census. Pocket guides are available with information on child well being for Asian-

American Children NEW!, American-Indian Children NEW!, Latino Children and African American Children. Order hard copies of the guides.

2/4/04 Casey Connects is a newsletter that reports on current activities of the Foundation and its grantees. The Spring/Summer issue highlights the release of the 2004 KIDS COUNT Data Book and the challenges of helping "disconnected youth" make a successful transition to adulthood. It describes efforts to address the needs of young people who have spent time in foster care or the juvenile justice system, have become parents as teenagers, or have never finished high school. It also looks at initiatives to help young people assume leadership roles in their communities. Past issues are also available.

6/30/04 Five Organizations Named 2004 FAMILIES COUNT Honorees The Foundation is pleased to announce the 2004 FAMILIES COUNT National honorees. We recognize these remarkable organizations for connecting families to the support, opportunities and resources they need to thrive in tough neighborhoods. Each organization receives an unrestricted award of $500,000 and becomes part of the FAMILIES COUNT network. Learn more about the 2004 honorees and FAMILIES COUNT: THE NATIONAL HONORS.

11/23/03   Annie E. Casey Foundation: The Casey Foundation makes grants, funds demonstrations, provides services and disseminates data and analysis aimed at helping states, cities, and neighborhoods support children and families.

Bill and Melinda Gates Foundation: The Gates Foundation assists public libraries in ensuring community access to the Internet, and training library personnel in the use of emerging communications technologies. Here is just a small sample of what this Foundation does and if they would only focus a small portion of their charitable endowments to the African and African American male Digital Divide issue the problem would be resolved. Below is just a small sample of what the Foundation did this year.

6/30/04 American Red Cross-$233,780 over 1 year to procure and distribute essential relief items to affected families in the Dominican Republic and Haiti where widespread flooding has occurred.

6/10/04 Global Partnerships-$100,000 over 1 year to support Phase II in the Seattle Initiative for Global Development.

6/10/04 International Society for Equity in Health ISEqH-$50,000 over 1 year to provide a forum for scientific interchange around health equity research, foster discussion around policies and policy implementation and establish an African regional network.

6/7/04 Treatment Action Group-$979,189 over 2 years to strengthen domestic and international HIV community responses to TB-HIV co-infection in partnership with community representatives from high-burden countries.

6/7/04 University of Tuebingen-$765,200 over 4 years to provide intermittent sulfadoxine-pyrimethamine administration to infants to reduce morbidity in Gabon Africa.

6/4/04 Johns Hopkins University-$44,651,305 over 7 years to develop and validate novel, community-level intervention strategies to reduce rates of tuberculosis in populations with epidemic rates of HIV infection and escalating tuberculosis incidence.

6/3/04 Center for Global Development-$1,610,000 over 1 year to fund Policy Research Network Working Groups and related activities.

6/1/04 Columbia University Earth Institute-$500,000 over 19 months to demonstrate the importance of sexual and reproductive health (SRH) to the achievement of the MDGs and to help ensure the incorporation and operationalization of the SRH in national poverty reduction strategies.

5/25/04 Family Health International-$1,515,721 over 5 years to strengthen the internal mobilization and organizing capability of the network of HIV positive people, to effectively advocate for the reduction of stigma and discrimination, ultimately resulting in a supportive environment.

5/25/04 Institute for One World Health-$1,429,611 over 1 year to support the development of an attenuated Plasmodium falciparum sporozoite vaccine to reduce malaria infection, morbidity, and mortality.

5/20/04 National Institutes of Health-$2,715,000 over 5 years (DCPP -- Phase II) to reduce death, illness, and disability in developing countries by providing authoritative information on improving resource allocation to cost-effective health interventions.

5/20/04 World Health Organization-$710,000 over 4 years to improve access to essential reproductive health medicines and commodities, by promoting global standards, developing guidance on good-quality suppliers and building procurement capacity in resource-limited countries (Phase I).

5/19/04 Yale University School of Medicine-$2,106,289 over 3 years to implement structural interventions for HIV prevention among high-risk groups in Andhra Pradesh, Karnataka, Tamil Nadu and Maharashtra India.

5/18/04 Family Care International-$601,000 over 1 year to assess progress toward the ICPD goals, produce a comprehensive policy and recommendations, and to raise awareness in the international community.

5/17/04 CARE-$6,703,648 over 5 years to increase leadership and improve enabling and learning environment for effective HIV/STI prevention and care in India.

5/14/04 United States Fund for UNICEF-$500,000 over 4 months to reduce child mortality in the Darfur region of Sudan through the control and elimination of measles infection by providing immunization.

5/11/04 Fundacio Clinic per a la Recerca Biomedica-$3,975,116 over 5 years to support components of an Intermittent Preventive Treatment of Infants (IPTi) project focused on cost-effectiveness and a clinical and immunological rebound study of IPTi.

5/3/04 University of Iowa-$50,000 over 1 year to support the 14th International Pathogenic Neisseria Conference.

4/29/04 International Rescue Committee-$500,000 over 1 year to provide humanitarian assistance to internally displaced people in Darfur, Sudan. 2004 International Crisis Group $250,000 over 1 year to support an intensive effort aimed at the immediate action of preventing a humanitarian catastrophe in Darfur.

California Wellness Foundation: CWF provides grants for California-based organizations dedicated to improving community health. If this Foundation decided to end the African and African American Digital Divide issue and focused primarily on this issue until it was resolved conquering this issue then move on to the next there would be a much greater impact on problem resolutions and the world would be much better off. Here is more information on what this Foundation does: The Foundation prioritizes eight issues for funding and responds to timely issues or special projects outside the funding priorities.   They encourage requests for core operating support, but requests for project funding are also welcome. Core operating support can be used to help underwrite the regular, ongoing health promotion and disease prevention activities of your organization.   Such funds can also be used to strengthen organizational infrastructure through activities such as providing salaries for key administrative staff, covering operating expenses, engaging in strategic planning or facilitating board development. No one private foundation, no matter how large, can begin to address all of the factors that affect health across a state as complex as California. We must make choices about the most effective use of grant dollars and human resources.

Because they believe there is no single definition of strategic philanthropy, they are committed to funding work at several levels. At least half of our grant making each year is for direct preventive health services.

Finding the combination of funding strategies that makes the greatest impact is a challenge all foundations face. The California Wellness Foundation has been known for its proactive, project-driven initiatives. While they believe these programs have had positive outcomes, they realized they had to do more to invest in the basic organizational needs of nonprofit organizations. That's why their board of directors decided that, beginning in July 2001, their emphasis would be on providing core-operating support, otherwise known as unrestricted funding. Kellogg Foundation's Managing Information with Rural America: grants to help people in rural communities determine how technology can be used to address economic development, education, health and leadership. This Foundation has many, many projects related to rural access to technologies. If they would focus only on the most needy at this time there would a greater sense of achievement.

National Cristina Foundation: This group provides computer technology and training for people with disabilities, students at risk and economically disadvantaged persons. Again, if this Foundation had focused their resources on all of the African and African American male there would be a greater impact on society.

Foundations both publicly sponsored and privately sponsored have practically unlimited resources, (especially the ones mentioned above), and the African and African American male Digital Divide problem could be easily resolved by any one of these Foundations or corporations if they would turn all of their energy and resources onto the issue. The impact in resolving this one problem for all of the African and African American males would allow more African American males to contribute rather than be considered social refugees waiting for help to overcome this prejudicial issue.

Chapter 10

African and African American Technology Achievers

African and African American males' are in dire need of role models' to let them believe that it is possible for them to achieve with technology and that technology is and always has been essential to be successful in life. There are countless African and African American inventions that have contributed largely to the White mans' current modern and luxurious lifestyle. The African and African American male needs to find his niche in life and exploit it for his own benefit and the best and most suitable method of finding that niche is through technology. Below I have listed several African and African American inventors' who literally brought White people as well as their selves into a bright and wonderful technological dream.

Lewis Howard Latimer

Lewis Howard Latimer (1848-1928) was an inventor and scientist who was born in Chelsea, Mass. and had served in the Union Navy in 1863. He studied drafting, and in 1881 invented and patented an incandescent light bulb with a carbon filament. He served for the Edison Company as an engineer for an extended period of time, and while serving he supervised the installation of the electric light systems in New York, N.Y., Montreal, Canada, London, England and Philadelphia, Pa. It was Latimer's job as well to write the first textbook on the lighting system used by the Edison Company. He also was employed by Alexander Graham Bell where he made patent drawings for the first telephone invented. Other position he served as include chief draftsman for General Electric and Westinghouse companies.

Lewis Latimer was an accomplished poet, painter, play write, musician and of course engineer. He was able to leap many hurdles that others were unable to. Thomas Edison's bamboo filament was impractical burning for only 30 hours before burning out. To overcome this problem Latimer invented the carbon filament, which made the light bulb practical.

So, the next time you stare out at the beautiful holiday lighted seasonal decorations, pay homage to the man who made the light bulb practical and available to us all; Lewis Howard Latimer. References: Low and Clift, The Encyclopedia of Black America.

Elijah McCoy

Elijah McCoy lived between the years 1843–1929 and was most famous for inventing a device that lubricated steam engines while the engine was running, (an oil-dripping cup). The son of former slaves, he was born in

Colchester, Ontario, Canada on May 2, 1844. His family had fled from Kentucky before the U.S. Civil War had begun. He was educated in Scotland as a mechanical engineer and after finishing Elijah McCoy returned to the United States and settled in Detroit, Michigan. There he began experimenting with a cup that would regulate the flow of oil onto moving parts of industrial machines and thusly lubricating them while the machines were in motion.

The lubricator for steam engines was his first invention U.S. patent #129,843, which was issued on July 12, 1872. The invention allowed machines to be oiled while they were running. This new oiling device completely revolutionized the industrial machine industry. Elijah McCoy started his own business, which was responsible for a total of 57 patents and is where the term "real McCoy" is derived referring to the original or real thing. The lubricating device became so popular and so associated with his name that people inspecting new equipment would ask if the device contained the real McCoy helping to make in vogue the American expression, meaning the real thing. McCoy also invented the ironing board and lawn sprinkler.

Elijah McCoy died on October 10, 1929 after a year in the Eloise Infirmary, Eloise, Michigan, suffering from senile dementia caused by hypertension. He was buried in Detroit, Michigan.

Professional Title: Vice-President, McCoy Manufacturing Company, Detroit, Michigan.

Bibliography:

Afro-American Encyclopedia, volume VI

Martin Rywell (chief compiler) and Charles H. Wesley, et al. (North Miami, FL: Educational Book Publishers), 1974. p. 617.

Afro USA: A Reference Work on the Black Experience.

Harry A. Ploski and Ernest Kaiser. (New York, NY: Bellwether Publishing Co., Distributed by Afro American Press), 1971, p. 732 At Last Recognition in America: A Reference Handbook of Unknown Black Inventors and their

Contribution to America, v. 1, James C. Williams, compiler. (Chicago, IL: BCA Publishing Co.), 1978. p. 31-32.

Dictionary of American Biography.

(New York: Scribner's), 1964. Volume 11, Part 1, p. 617.

Dictionary of American Negro Biography.

Rayford W. Logan and Michael R. Winston, editors. (New York: Norton), 1982. p. 413-141.

Great Negroes, Past and Present. Russell L. Adams. Illustrated by Eugene Winslow. Edited by David P. Ross, Jr. (Chicago, Afro-Am Pub. Co.), 1969. p. 61.

Negro Almanac. (New York: Bellwether Pub. Co.), p. 639.

Negro in Our History. 5th ed., Carter Godwin Woodson. (Washington, D.C.: The Associated Publishers, Inc.), 1928. p. 465-566 The Role of the American Negro in the Fields of Science.

Louis Haber. (New York), 1966. p. 17-18. Who Was Who in American History-Science And Technology: A Component of Who's Who in American History. (Chicago: Marquis Who's Who), 1976. p. 400.

Jan Ernst Matzeliger

Jan Ernst Matzeliger lived between the ages of 1852–1889 and is know for inventing a shoe-making machine that increased shoe-making speed by 900%! He was born in Dutch Guiana, South America and was ultimately to create an important invention that the corporation that manufactured it has grown to a present-day worth of over a billion dollars. From a Dutch father/engineer and am mother of African and Surinamese decent, through his father's guidance, his mechanical aptitude was carefully nurtured and his agility with his hands became readily apparent.

1871 was the year that Jan started a voyage and then later settled in Lynn, Massachusetts, where he works in a shoe factory in 1877. At that time, every stage of the shoe manufacturing process was done by machine except for the last step, which was sewing the upper portion of the shoe to the sole around a plaster cast of the purchasers' foot.

Using this plaster cast method was so labor-intensive that it resulted in the production of only fifty shoes per day. Shoe lasters were very important at the time because only skilled human hands could complete the final process of shoe manufacture. Jan's idea of a machine being able to tack and sew the components together was laughed at by friends and scoffed at by co-workers. Unwaveringly, Jan began to experiment as he observed their shoemaking techniques and by 1880, with wood, wire, and cigar boxes, Matzeliger developed the prototype "Lasting Machine" and then came a complex metal design whose drawings were submitted to the U.S. Patent Office who sent a scientist to review the inventions operation. A revolution in the shoe industry had begun when on March 20, 1883, Matzeliger received Patent No. 274,207 for the Lasting Machine.

In a public demonstration on May 29, 1885, he made seventy-five shoes by machine in one day. With improvements production soared from 150 to 700 shoes per day. Matzeliger further received patents for "Mechanism for

Distributing Tacks", "Nailing Machine", and the "Tack Separating Machine". In 1889, the Consolidated Lasting Machine Company was formed with Matzeliger retaining stock in his inventions. Its corporate heirs are now worth more than one billion dollars. All shoes manufactured by machine today use the Matzeliger principles for lasting.

Matzeliger never married and was a devout Christian and at the young age of thirty-seven, he died of tuberculosis leaving substantial stock to his church.

The First Church of Christ honored him posthumously in 1967 and a statue of him was placed in downtown Lynn and also the U.S. Post Office issued a stamp recognizing his achievements in 1992.

Granville T. Woods

Granville T. Woods lived between 1856–1910 and invented a train-to-station communication system.

In the 1880s trains operated smoothly, thanks to the lubricating devices of Elijah McCoy, yet unfortunately, there were still many wrecks because unscheduled trains often criss-crossed each other. The locomotive engineers did not have a way to communicate with each other--until the genius of Granville T. Woods came to their rescue. In the year 1887 Woods invented the induction telegraphy system that allowed each engineer to communicate instantly with other moving trains allowing the trains to run smoothly and safely.

Hailed by White electricians as "the best electrical engineer in the world", Woods was a prolific inventor. Beginning in 1884 with his steam-boiler furnace, he continued on in 1888 with a method to supply current to a locomotive or a car through a wire overhead, sending the current down from a small grooved wheel which Woods called a "troller". This invention and name became attached to the car that later became "trolley car". In 1891, Woods invented the electric railway system.

When Woods moved from Ohio to New York City, he invented a chicken incubator, which set the principles in use today for incubating thousands of eggs at the same time and during that same period, Woods invented the "third rail", now used by subway systems.

Woods holds twenty-three patents including an improved telephone transmitter that he sold to Bell Telephone Company; a telephone system and apparatus; tunnel construction for electric railway; electro-motive railway system; and an electric railway supply apparatus and an amusement apparatus.

Elijah McCoy and Woods held fifty patents during the period between 1871 and 1900. During that same period African Americans held more than 400 patents. Unfortunately there were hundreds of patents that were not issued to them. Woods, like so many other African and African American geniuses, was stripped of his money. Thomas Edison and Lucius Phelps laid claim, in court, to having invented the induction telegraph although it was obvious that Woods' invention preceded theirs by years, Woods had to spend large sums of money in legal fees for his defense.

Sadly, another African American male died with no legacy for his children.

George Washington Carver

George Washington Carver who lived between the years 1860 and 1943 invented peanut butter and 400 plant products! He was born on a farm near Diamond, Missouri and received a B.S. from the Iowa Agricultural College in 1894 and a M.S. in 1896 and became a member of the faculty of Iowa State College of Agriculture and Mechanic Arts in charge of the schools bacterial laboratory work in the Systematic Botany department. Carver's experimentation with agricultural products developed a science called chemurgy, which is finding industrial applications for farm products through experimentation. His research developed 325 products from peanuts, 108 applications for sweet potatoes, and 75 products derived from pecans. He accepted a position in 1896 as an instructor at the Tuskegee Normal and Industrial Institute and remained on the faculty until his death in 1943. His work in developing industrial applications from agricultural products derived 118 products, including a rubber substitute and over 500 dyes and pigments, from 28 different plants. He was responsible for the invention in 1927 of a process for producing paints and stains from soybeans, for which three separate patents were issued.

George Washington Carver was honored by U.S. President Franklin Delano Roosevelt in July 14, 1943 dedicating $30,000 for a national monument to be dedicated to his accomplishments. The area of Carver's childhood near Diamond, Missouri has been preserved as a park, with a bust of the agricultural researcher, instructor, and chemical investigator. This park was the first designated national monument to an African American in the United States. George Washington Carver was bestowed an honorary doctorate from Simpson College in 1928. He was made a member of the Royal Society of Arts in London, England. He received the Spingarn Medal in 1923, which is given every year by the National Association for the

Advancement of colored People. The Spingarn Medal is awarded to the African American person who has made the greatest contribution to the advancement of his race. Carver died of anemia at Tuskegee Institute on January 5, 1943 and was buried on campus beside Booker T. Washington. (DNB, p.95) Some of the synthetic products developed by Dr. Carver:

Adhesives, Axle Grease, Bleach, Buttermilk, Cheese, Chili Sauce, Cream, Creosote, Dyes, Flour, Fuel, Briquettes, Ink, Instant Coffee, Insulating Board, Linoleum, Mayonnaise, Meal, Meat Tenderizer, Metal Polish, Milk Flakes, Mucilage, Paper, Rubbing Oils, Salve, Soil Conditioner, Shampoo, Shoe Polish, Shaving Cream, Sugar, Synthetic Marble, Synthetic Rubber, Talcum Powder, Vanishing Cream, Wood Stains, Wood Filler, and Worcestershire Sauce.

   * Source: Hattie Carwell. Blacks in Science: Astrophysicist to Zoologist.

(Hicksville, N.Y.: Exposition Press), 1977. p. 18.

Source: Linda McMurray. George Washington Carver. (New York, NY: Oxford University Press), 1981.

For a lengthy discussion of the controversy of Carver's birth date. Anna Coxe Toogood. Historic Resource Study and Administrative History, George Washington Carver National Monument, Diamond, Missouri (Denver, 1973), pp. 8-21.

Garrett Morgan

Garrett Morgan lived between the years 1877–1963 and he invented the gas mask.

He was born in Paris, Kentucky, on March 4, 1877 and later moved to Cleveland where he spent most of his youth. Morgan deserves credit for playing an integral role in the shaping of America. One day he witnessed a two-car collision on a main intersection where two people were badly injured and the driver rendered unconscious. Morgan pondered the dilemma for a while and later devised the method that would eliminate the problem and he invented the three-color traffic signal, which ultimately became what is commonly known as the traffic light and sold the patent rights to General Electric for $40,000.

Some of his inventions include: a woman's hat fastener, a round belt fastener, and a friction drive belt.

Morgan sharpened his skill and expertise-increasing acuity, which allowed him to open a tailoring shop manufacturing, dresses, suits and, coats. The first human-hair straightener that was marketed as the G. A. Morgan Hair Refining Cream was developed in this shop.

The invention that proved the prominence of his genius was his invention of the gas mask in 1912 that was a device that consisted of a hood placed over the users' head. The gas mask consisted of a tube from the hood that provided an inlet opening for air to reach the gas mask wearer. There was a tunnel explosion that occurred after the gas masks development that gave Morgan and his brother Frank a chance to exhibit the device, which as it turned out were extremely heroic rescues. The rescues made all of the newspapers although it also showed that the inventors were African American that led to acts of discrimination.

Orders poured in from all over the United States from coal mining and other companies that could utilize the gas mask however, when it was found out that the inventor was an African American, all orders were canceled. To overcome racial prejudice, Morgan first presented himself as Big Chief Mason, a Native American, which improved sales of the gas mask. The   White people in charge of ordering, including the United States Army, still refused to purchase the gas mask from an African American and therefore Morgan employed the services of a White man who pretended to be the inventor which Morgan had to pay a large part of the profits to.

World War I began and Morgan's gas inhalator was improved upon and the U.S. Army used it successfully on the battlefield to save thousands of lives.

Morgan lived to the age of 86 when he died after living with glaucoma for the last 2 years of his life. Morgan was a brilliant torchbearer who died on July 27, 1963.

Otis Boykin

Otis Boykin lived from 1920-1982 and was responsible for inventing many valuable items including the electronic control devices for guided missiles, IBM computers, and the pacemaker.

Otis Boykin was educated at Fisk University and Illinois Institute of Technology (1946-47). In addition to inventing the electrical device used in all guided missiles and IBM computers, and the pacemaker he invented 26 other electronic devices. He began his career as a laboratory assistant testing automatic controls for aircraft. Boykin's first achievement was the invention of a type of resistor used in computers, radios, television sets. Boykin's innovations in resistor design led to a reduced cost when producing electronic controls for radio and television and his designs were used for both military and commercial applications.

Otis Boykin also invented a burglarproof cash register and chemical air filter. From 1964 to 1982 he worked as a private consultant for several American firms and three Paris firms. Ironically, Otis Boykin died in Chicago, Illinois of heart failure in 1982.

Bibliography:

Afro Americans in Science and Invention.

Robert C. Hayden. "Afro Americans in Science and Invention", Journal of African Civilizations (November 1959): 59-72.

Biography Index. A cumulative index to biographical material in books and magazines.

(New York: H.W. Wilson Co.), 1995.

Volume 20: September, 1994-August, 1995

Black Contributors to Science and Energy Technology.

U.S. Department of Energy (Washington, D.C.: Office of Public Affairs), 1979, p. 12.

DOE/OPA-0035 (79) Blacks in Science and Medicine.

Vivian O. Sammons. (New York, NY: Hemisphere Publishing Corp.), 1990. p.34. Blacks in Science: Ancient and Modern.

Irvan Van Sertima. (New Brunswick, NJ: Transition Books), 1984. p. 226. In Black and White. A guide to magazine articles, newspaper articles, and books concerning Black individuals and groups. Third edition. Edited by Mary Mace Spradling. (Detroit: Gale Research), 1980.

Negro Almanac: A Reference Work of the Afro American. 4th ed. Harry A. Ploski and James Williams, eds. (New York, NY: Wiley), 1983. p. 1055.

Negro Almanac: A Reference Work of the Afro American. 4th ed. Harry A. Ploski and James Williams, eds. (New York, NY: Wiley), 1989. p.

Notable Black American Scientists. (Detroit: Gale Research), 1999.

Notable Twentieth-Century Scientists. First edition. (Detroit: Gale Research), 1995.

Who's Who in the Midwest. (Wilmette, IL: Marquis Who's Who) 16th edition, 1978-1979 17th edition, 1980-1981

World of Invention. History's most significant inventions and the people behind them. (Detroit: Gale Research), 1994.

Lonnie G. Johnson

Lonnie G. Johnson was born in the year 1949 and is responsible for inventing the world-famous water gun, the Supersoaker.

Lonnie G. Johnson normally worked as an inventor of thermodynamics systems for NASA and other organizations, but the invention he is most famous for is the Supersoaker squirt gun.

Johnson's love to tinker with appliance during his childhood eventually led to his winning a national inventing competition for "Linex", which was a remote-controlled robot he had built out of scraps from the junkyard. He then attended college at Tuskegee University, where he earned first a B.S. in Mechanical Engineering (1972) and then an M.S. in Nuclear Engineering (1974).

After graduation Johnson joined the U.S. Air Force where he became an Advanced Space Systems Requirements Officer at the headquarters of the Strategic Air Command in Omaha, Nebraska. Johnson directed a multitude of projects and earned several decorations and was nominated for astronaut training. Johnson moved on to NASA's Jet Propulsion Laboratory in California where he helped develop thermodynamic and control systems and did award-winning work for the Galileo Jupiter probe and the Mars Observer project. His most noteworthy invention at JPL was the Johnson Tube, a CFC-free refrigeration system with a hydraulic heat pump, which later earned Johnson his seventh patent (#4,724,683; 1988).

While with the USAF and JPL, Johnson continued to invent at home. In 1985, he founded his own company, later renamed Johnson Research and Development.

Johnson had first conceived his Supersoaker invention in 1982 and it turned out to be the world's first high-performance, pressurized water gun.

Johnson worked with partner Bruce D'Andrade and created a workable prototype of the now famous SuperSoaker® in 1989. They were granted a patent for the device in 1991 and found a manufacturer, Larami Corp. The SuperSoaker® uses an air pump to pressurize its water supply, allowing for tremendous distance and accuracy in water-marksmanship. This invention has generated over $200 million dollars in sales and is still a very popular toy.

In his lifetime, Johnson has earned over 40 patents. He continues to invent toys and also invents items in the thermo and fluid dynamics area of engineering science. In addition to ongoing controls work for NASA and his company is also improving technology various areas of heating and cooling equipment and electronics.

Lonnie Johnson is a hero to kids nationwide and has won multiple honors for inventing and entrepreneurship, and his favorable example as a role model that encourages young people to turn their ideas into inventions. Johnson's hometown, Marietta, Georgia declared February 25th, 1994 as "Lonnie G. Johnson Day".

http://web.mit.edu/invent/iow/johnson.html   [Sept. 1998]

Chapter 11

World Wide Access Issues

World Wide Access to (ICT) or Information and Communication Technology is a matter of focus among societies and countries working to achieve this miraculous and monumental goal. There are currently projects planned whose purpose is to link Africa with Europe and the rest of the world through underwater fibre-optic cables and satellite networks to provide Africa with World Access to ICT, thusly reducing the expense of advanced networking and digital technology. Parts of Africa, primarily the western coastal region from Senegal to South Africa already are connected through underwater cables. Africa's east coast has no underwater fibre-optic cable therefore leaving the majority of the continent with international access available only through very expensive satellite technology. Currently, the east coast of Africa is the only coast in the world without an underwater fibre-optic cable making digital technology extremely expensive and also leaving large areas of Africa without communication technology. Africa needs access to this technology now.

The world is faced with Issues as to whether one country will share access with other countries based upon social acclimation, financial importance, and territorial boundaries. Many countries are endorsing legislation regarding World Wide Access including everything from state sponsored access for people with disabilities to laws regarding the control of information. Now is a great time for all countries to endorse legislation that will provide the technology for Internet access for one of the most digitally disparaged groups in the entire world, that group being the African and African American male.

Wireless technology is thought to be the answer to the Web's access in areas of the planet that are not wired for Web accessibility. The African and African American male needs access to this technology immediately for many reasons. He needs access to improve his chances of getting a higher education now, instead of waiting for some government implementation of a plan that might take decades to complete. African and African American males' need this technology to help them be part of state of the art service to those countries that are in need of and willing to pay high salaries to individuals who are trained in the use of technology. Internet businesses are currently providing substantial incomes to those lucky White people who have the technology in their homes and operating lucrative online stores. People with technology are able to check online for information regarding jobs in foreign countries. It is thought that if African and African

American people were technically enabled the spread of disease and famine and war would be cut off before it is too late rather then waiting until it is out of control. Since the world is so separated, only sparse communication at very best is available to many African and African American people. The technology to connect these people is available now so why not save lives by providing the technology for those who are in desperate need of it.

In the more sophisticated countries that are predominantly under the majorital control of White people there is a large amount of free Internet access available through several Internet companies. Most of these free Internet access companies thrive on advertising rather then charging the user a monthly access fee or perhaps they are sponsored by a government or private group. Europe has made available free Internet access longer than the United States and other countries. In the United States most Internet subscribers must pay a small monthly fee for a telephone connection to take advantage of a free Internet service, however, in Great Britain the user must still pay for the local phone call (usually on a per-minute basis) so the longer the user stays connected, the more that he or she will pay in phone costs. Internet usage in the United States is far less expensive than that in Great Britain.

Many of the same providers of free Internet access in the United States also are providers of service to Canada. India also has one free Internet service provider and they are attempting to start up a second one in the near future. Asia is also working on starting up free Internet access however at this time they do not have a free Internet service provider.

Some of the pitfalls of free Internet access companies in the United States and Canada are that they primarily service only major metropolitan areas. Also there are connectivity issues where if many users are trying to connect at the same time it is difficult to get connected and also many of the free Internet service providers went belly up when the stock market fell in the United States in the year 2000 so there are not as many free Internet service providers available as there used to be.

Free Internet access at local libraries is available and of course that could have time and use restrictions which conflict with the normal advantage that occurs while using an Internet connection at home.

World wide free Internet access would most certainly be a wonderful asset for the African and African American male.   There are programs offering free computer equipment such as the ones mentioned in previous chapters however these programs are still too sparse and are not focused directly on the African and African American male who is in most desperate need.

Below are some Internet links with more information on worldwide access to the Internet and also free Internet service providers.

http://www.olywa.net/blame/freenet1.htm

http://www.zdnet.com/anchordesk/talkback/talkback 222246.html Directories http://nzlist.org/user/freeisp/ has a comprehensive list of USA freenets, plus other free and low-cost ISP's http://www.y4i.com/freeaccess2.html lists freenets around the world.

http://www.emailaddresses.com/email_internet.htm doesn't list as many ISP's, but provides a more detailed review of those that it does list; including user comments; and it lists ISP's in Europe, Canada, Israel and South Africa, as well as the USA.

http://freeisps.4mg.com/ also lists free ISP's around the world.

http://thelist.internet.com/ is a list of all ISP's (or at least 8,500 of them) by area code.

http://www.freesiteuk.co.uk/ispcallcont.html lists free UK ISP's.

http://freeguysfreebies.tripod.com/freeisps.htm has a small list of ISP's, but some of them are not listed elsewhere — and they are rated.

http://www.olywa.net/blame/free/internet.htm is the list from Brett McCarron, the author of one of the best overviews of free-access (listed above).

Below are some free ISP's that have some special aspect, like Canadian availability or Macintosh compatibility.

PC (meaning IBM or compatible, instead of Macintosh) free access services: U.S. and Canada. Altavista Microportal is also one of the top-reviewed free-access services: http://microav.com/

Freewwweb http://www.freewwweb.com/ no longer charges a setup fee

http://www.freewebcanada.com.Freeweb Canada also has US access

Freelane http://freelane.excite.com/freelane/

http://www.cymo.com/freeaccess.htm

1stUp.com http://www.1stup.com includes over 50 co-branded ISP's: the same provider is offered through Lycos Free ISP http://lycos.1stup.com/help/system.html and Senior.com   http://cobrand.1stup.com/fcgibin/cobrand/cust_download?subpartner_id=7and   Idaho's

News Channel http://www.ktvb.net/

http://www.collegeclub.com/freeisp/   join   the

international College Club chat community, free, to qualify

for free ISP service offered by Spinway, which also powers

http://www.bluelight.com/ and http://www.address.com/

The television show the Simpsons offers free internet

access   at   http://www.thesimpsons.com/frameset.html?

content=/index.html

Canada only: http://www.3web.net/

U.S. Only

Worldspy promises no banner ads

http://worldspy.com/freeisp/isp.htm

http://www.dialfree.net/ also   offers   ad-free   service

http://www.freei.net/ is compatible with both Windows

and Mac and is one of the top-reviewed free ISP's StartFree

allows you your choice of browser (most others require you

to use IE) http://www.startfree.com/

The Broadband Digital Group offers high-speed access: http://www.freedsl.com/http://freeisp.xoom.com/ is a free ISP service from one of the largest and oldest free web space providers, and includes 500MB of online storage.

NetZero has directions in both English and Spanish http://www.netzero.net/

Juno, one of the oldest free-access providers, provides free Internet access and basic email service, U.S. Only and has now merged with Netzero. Expanded services, including browser capability and web space, are inexpensive. http://home.juno.com/corp/about/free.html

http://www.freensafe.com/ is a "family safe" service http://www.internetcomplete.com/ provides a package deal for the PC for a one-time cost of $179.95 --- the same service as at http://www.webcombo.net/ (Includes mainland U.S., Hawaii, Alaska and Puerto Rico) Macintosh: There are less free-access offers for Macintosh users, but they are growing: http://www.dialfree.net/ offers ad-free service U.S. Only Freewwweb http://home.freewwweb.

com/ no longer charges a setup fee (U.S. and Canada access) Freeweb Canada also has US access http://www.freewebcanada.com/ http://www.freei.net/ is compatible with both Windows and Mac — U.S.Only one of the top-reviewed free ISP's http://www.intern etcomplete.com/ provides a package deal for the Mac for a one-time cost of $199.95 - the same service as at http://www.webcombo.net/ (U.S. Only, includes Hawaii, Alaska and Puerto Rico) Freelane http://freelane. excite.com/freelane/ promises a Mac service soon (U.S. and Canada access) NetZero http://www.netzero.net/ also promises Mac support eventually to encourage them, write to macdemand@netzero.net (U.S. Only) UK residents only:

http://www.freebeeb.net/radiotimes/index.shtml

http://www.freeserve.net/myfreeserve/

Here is a portal page with pointers to email service, webspace, search engines and other Net uses: http://www.scn.org/~alf1701/portal/index.html

Public access to the Internet is available at libraries, community centers and colleges. To have a computer in one's home, one must have a personal computer with a modem and a live telephone connection. The African and African American male is in dire need of more resources then what are available at this time in order to enjoy success in his life and the key to helping him is focusing directly on his issues and applying resources that are currently being scattered ineffectively.

Chapter 12

New Technology

Wireless technology is currently considered state of the art for Internet access. Pocket PC's and other handhold gadgets allow for Internet access through the cellular and satellite communications system. Microwave systems have been in use by civilian and military contractors in remote areas for almost two decades allowing access to telephone and the Internet for the past decade. Personal computers are extremely fast and inexpensive to purchase. Internet access is available and is available very inexpensively as well.

Voice recognition is one of the latest advances. Voice recognition has been around for quite some time though until recently personal computers did not have the power to make it practical or state of the art. Voice recognition may be of benefit to the African and African American male as since he is currently so technically impeded he will be able to use his voice to write with a word processor rather then having to learn to type with his hands and fingers. Also, the new voice technology allows for voice commands to be given to the computer to turn it off and on and to open and use various software applications and this too is becoming state of the art.

Smart digital cameras attached or built-in to the computer can identify the person who is using it and can make it easy and fun to communicate with students and teachers over the PC. High-speed broadband Internet connections allow for instantaneous viewing of video and sound making it seem like the person is in the same room as the viewer. Internet connections are available at most public coffee houses and bookstores and wireless internet is available throughout most of the United States and Europe and the rest of the world.

Technology is constantly improving and now it is so inexpensive that African and African American males' should be given the equipment and access to improve their digitally disparaged life and to provide them with the same digital opportunities that are afforded to others of predominantly white persuasion.

Current research shows that low income African and African American boys perform far below the majority of their peers academically and much of this is due to his lack of access to technology. Technology would provide them with a place to play and learn at the same time. It would give them the advantages of being able to research and complete their school work with home computers rather then having to wait in line to use a public access computer system at the library or school. A personal computer in his home would allow him to explore the Internet and to explore new worlds and to have the same advantages that other people have and make him digitally equal providing him with the tools and opportunities he needs to improve his life.

Chapter 13

Conclusion

African and African American males are a group of people that have been tread upon for centuries. Truth discovered normally leads to justice yet regarding their gap in the Digital Divide truth has led the African and African American male only to more prejudice. African and African American males' need to function productively, and therefore as citizens of the world we must unite to aid them in their plight. New programs with the specific purpose of helping the African and African American male must begin now and at the global level.

Economic and social disparities are pressuring the African and African American male into higher levels of destructive and anti-social behavior not seen in other groups. Digital equality is one of the many ways the world can help these people improve their financial and social situations and to help them find hope in leading as good a life as any.

Here is a quote from the book, Powershift, by Alvin and Heidi Toffler where they warn that a shift is coming that will allow for wealth of information to exert more control over the world then financial wealth or military strength. In their book they warn of the technology chasm that separates the armed from the unarmed and the ignorant from the educated. Despite all inequities of income and wealth, the coming struggle for power will increasingly turn into a struggle over the distribution of and access to knowledge. The African and African American male needs priority and preferential treatment. There is an urgent need for technologically gifted organizations to step in and assist them. Government programs are all aimed to help with immediate needs and go little further then providing food and shelter for the general needy public.   Worldwide, lawmakers and providers of support for private and publicly funded programs must bring the African and African American male to the very top of their lists when it comes to providing resources to fight the Digital Divide.

Philanthropical support is normally too generalized and in need of focus and the focus needs to be placed on the African and African American male who has been left behind long enough.

REFERENCES

- 17th edition, 1980-1981 World of Invention. History's most significant inventions and the people behind them. (Detroit: Gale Research), 1994.

- Afro USA: A Reference Work on the Black Experience. Harry A. Ploski and Ernest Kaiser.(New York, NY: Bellwether Publishing Co., Distributed by Afro American Press), 1971, p.732.

- Afro-American Encyclopedia, volume VI Martin Rywell (chief compiler) and Charles H. Wesley, et al. (North Miami, FL: Educational Book Publishers), 1974. p. 617.

- Anna Coxe Toogood. Historic Resource Study and Administrative History, George Washington Carver National Monument, Diamond, Missouri (Denver, 1973), pp. 8-21.

- At Last Recognition in America: A Reference Handbook of Unknown Black Inventors and their Contribution to America., v. 1, James C. Williams, compiler. (Chicago, IL: BCA Publishing Co.), 1978. p. 31-32.

- Biography Index. A cumulative index to biographical material in books and magazines. (New York: H.W. Wilson Co.), 1995. Volume 20: September, 1994-August, 1995.

- Black Contributors to Science and Energy Technology. U.S. Department of Energy (Washington, D.C.: Office of Public Affairs), 1979, p. 12. DOE/OPA-0035(79).

- Black individuals and groups. Third edition. Edited by Mary Mace Spradling. (Detroit: Gale Research), 1980.

- Blacks in Science and Medicine. Vivian O. Sammons. (New York, NY: Hemisphere Publishing Corp.),   1990. p.34.

- Blacks in Science: Ancient and Modern. Irvan Van Sertima. (New Brunswick, NJ: Transition Books), 1984. p. 226.

- Dictionary of American Biography. (New York : Scribner's), 1964. Volume 11, Part 1, p. 617.

- Dictionary of American Negro Biography. Rayford W. Logan and Michael R. Winston, editors. (New York: Norton), 1982. p. 413-141.

- Gibbs, T., "Young, black, and male in American: and endangered species" Auburn House Pub. Co., 1988. Dover, Mass.

- Great Negroes, Past and Present. Russell L. Adams. Illustrated by Eugene Winslow. Edited by David P. Ross, Jr. (Chicago, Afro-Am Pub. Co.), 1969. p. 61.

- Hattie Carwell. Blacks in Science: Astrophysicist to Zoologist. (Hicksville, N.Y.: Exposition Press), 1977. p. 18.

- Hoffman, D., Novak, T., Schlosser, A. "The Evolution of the Digital Divide: How Gaps in Internet Access May Impact Electronic Commerce" Owen Graduate School of Management Vanderbilt University March, 2000 http://jcmc.indiana.edu/ vol5/issue3/hoffman.html

- Http://web.mit.edu/invent/iow/johnson.html [Sept. 1998]

- In Black and White. A guide to magazine articles, newspaper articles, and books concerning.

- Knapp, S. "New study: Interracial interactions are cognitively demanding" Dartmouth News. 17 November, 2003 http://www.dartmouth.edu/~news/releases/2003/11/17.html

- Linda McMurray. George Washington Carver. (New York, NY: Oxford University Press), 1981.

- Low, A., Clift, V. "Encyclopedia of Black America" Da Capo August 1984

- McConnaughey, J., Lader, W. "Falling Through the Net II: New Data on the Digital Divide" National Telecommunications and Information Administration February, 1998 http://www.ntia.doc.gov/ntiahome/net2/falling.html

- Negro Almanac. (New York : Bellwether Pub. Co.), p. 639.

- Negro Almanac: A Reference Work of the Afro American. 4th ed. Harry A. Ploski and James Williams, eds. (New York, NY: Wiley), 1983. p. 1055.

- Negro Almanac: A Reference Work of the Afro American. 4th ed. Harry A. Ploski and James Williams, eds. (New York, NY: Wiley), 1989. p. 1112.

- Negro in Our History. 5th ed., Carter Godwin Woodson. (Washington, D.C.: The Associated Publishers, Inc.), 1928. p. 465-566.

- Notable Black American Scientists. (Detroit: Gale Research), 1999.

- Notable Twentieth-Century Scientists. First edition. (Detroit: Gale Research), 1995.

- Robert C. Hayden. "Afro Americans in Science and Invention", Journal of African Civilizations (November 1959): 59-72.

- The Henry J. Kaiser Family Foundation, "Survey Shows Widespread Enthusiasm for High Technology?" The Henry J. Kaiser Family Foundation 29 February, 2000 http://www.kff.org/entmedia/upload/New-V-Chip-and-TV-Ratings-Study-Release-Summary-of-Findings.pdf

- The Role of the American Negro in the Fields of Science. Louis Haber. (New York), 1966. p. 17-18.

- Valletta, Robert, G., Federal Reserve Bank of San Francisco, "The Computer Evolution" Federal Reserve Bank of San Francisco 8 April, 2005 http://66.218.69.11/search/cache?ei=UTF-8&p=the+ computer+evolution+bank+of+san+francisco&fr=slv8-msgr&u=www.frbsf.org/economics/economists/rvalletta /RVcomp-dist_4-05.pdf&w=computer+computers+ evolution+bank+san+Francisco&d=cfyW2OdmPbTP&icp =1&.intl=us

- Who Was Who in American History-Science And Technology : A Component of Who's Who in American History. (Chicago : Marquis Who's Who), 1976. p. 400.

- Who's Who in the Midwest. (Wilmette, IL: Marquis Who's Who) 16th edition, 1978-1979

INDEX

Printed in Great Britain
by Amazon

33081112R00130